TheThirdTeacher

The child

Every 29 seconds another student gives up in school, resulting in more than one million American high school students dropping out every year.

kinderga

In the U.S. alone, more than 59 million students, teachers, and education employees spend part of their day in schools.

fall will g

You can't expect children to learn 21st-century skills in schools built for the 1950s. We need schools designed for 21st-century success. —*Chad P. Wick, president and CEO, KnowledgeWorks Foundation*

in the thi

There are 97,382 public schools in the United States.

of the 21s

starting

ten this

aduate

d decade

t century.

All we can kno

We are currently preparing students for jobs that don't yet exist, using technologies that haven't yet been invented, in order to solve problems we don't even know are problems yet. —*Karl Fisch, educator*

world she will s

The world of children is imaginative play. Put two kids in the room together and all of a sudden they'll create something. —*Albert Cullum, educator*

it will have chal

The average British child's height and build is very different than that of a child in the 1960s, which is the last time children were actually measured for determining measures of furniture. —*Dominic Savage, director, British Educational Suppliers Association*

opportunities b

By 2013, spending on construction, renovation, and maintenance of U.S. schools is expected to total nearly $30 billion annually,

can imagine to

In 1998, the average public school building in the United States was 42 years old.

and possibilitie

A Victorian teacher would get the hang of a modern school quite easily. —*Sean McDougall, educational thinker and designer*

mand creativity

There are about 10 billion neurons in the brain and about 1,000 trillion connections. The possible combination of connections is about 10 to the one-millionth power. An enriched environment can contribute up to a 25% increase in the number of brain connections.

responsibility a

about the
ep into is that
enges and
eyond what we
lay, problems
that will de-
and ingenuity,
d compassion.

Whether this garten stude survive or po in the decad depends in l on the exper has in school

An estimated 25,000 schools throughout America need major repair or outright replacement, and 60% of all schools report at least one major building feature that needs replacement or extensive repairs.

Asthma is the leading cause of absenteeism, responsible for more than 20 million missed schools days in the U.S. per year.

83% of German primary school children sit at a chair-desk combination unsuited for their body height.

More than one in ten U.S. high schools are "Drop Out Factories" where no more than 60% of students who start as freshman make it to their senior year.

One-third of German children between the ages of seven and 17 report getting headaches at school.

To me, it's about recognizing that there is a much richer conception of intelligence and ability available to us than is promoted by conventional education. —*Sir Ken Robinson, creativity expert*

year's kinder-
t will merely
itively thrive
s to come
rge measure
ences she

Those exper

The best teachers emphasize their ability to control classroom temperature as central to the performance of teachers and students.

be shaped

Nearly half of all schools in the U.S. lack the basic electrical wiring to support computers, modems, and other communication technology.

peers, and u

In 2007, the public perception of schools in the U.S. was the lowest in recorded history.

places, by t

Five percent of elementary school students in Canada report being bullied 10 or more times a month.

environmen

Our education system looks a lot like the U.S. auto industry in the 1970s, stuck in a flabby, inefficient, outdated production model. —Michael Bloomberg, mayor of New York City

she does he

ences will

y adults, by

ltimately by

e physical

s where

r learning.

United in th

A study has shown that after installing an electromagnetic air cleaner in classrooms, absenteeism dropped from 8.3% to 3.7%. After the air purifier was removed, the rate jumped up to 7.9%.

that environ

U.S. national average for annual expenditures per student: $10,418.

children's thi

What should schools look like when information is loose and available everywhere in ways that are personally relevant and streamlined to individual students? —*Renate Nummela Caine and Geoffrey Caine, education consultants*

we can begi

What we want to see is the child in pursuit of knowledge, and not knowledge in pursuit of the child. —*George Bernard Shaw, playwright*

vital mission

A child miseducated is a child lost. —*John F. Kennedy, former president of the United States*

today's scho

And when they look around and see   that no one has lifted a finger to fix their school since the 19th century; when they are pushed out the door at the sound of the last bell ... is it any wonder they don't think their education is important? —*Barack Obama, president of the United States*

tomorrow's w

conviction
...ment is our
...d teacher,
...n anew a
...designing
...ols for
...orld.

The Third

79 Ways You Can Use Design t

OWP/P Architects
VS Furniture
Bruce Mau Design

Teacher

ansform Teaching & Learning

FOREWORD:
DAVID W. ORR

Learning is far more complicated than once thought but also far simpler than commonly presumed. The complications arise because learning involves more than just school, curriculum, and test results. It is, rather, the result of the complex interplay between the child's body, diet, family life, security, neighborhood, teachers, school, peers, access to information, and a great deal more. But learning is also simpler than educators armed with the latest curricular materials and quantitative studies sometimes presume. Children will always learn. They learn early on by play. They learn on the streets and in classrooms, they learn from peers and from teachers. They learn from television and Internet and from books. Sometimes they learn things we wish they had not learned. They learn to compete or cooperate, fear or trust, join or isolate, but they will learn—it's in their genes.

Children will create as well. Whether order or disorder, chaos or harmony, beauty or ugliness, accord or violence, they will create. We all begin life with a will to leave a mark that no one else has left. Creativity, too, is in our genes.

Humans are particularly plastic, shaped by experiences early in life. Aldo Leopold, for example, began a half-century conversation about the human role in nature as a child playing in the marshes along the Mississippi River. Edward O. ("Snake") Wilson began his lifelong love affair with animals as a child exploring nearby woods in Alabama. The stories are endless, but the point is the same. The best learning often occurs when children spend unplanned and uncounted hours outdoors investigating, experimenting, exploring, and playing—which is to say spontaneously and delightfully designing their own curriculum. In the right circumstances, the result is a lifelong love affair with birds, bugs, fish, plants, trees, water, seashore, and landscapes, a love affair that is the foundation for an imaginative life rich in possibilities.

I count it as one of the great tragedies of the modern world that sprawl and industrialization of landscapes have ruined many of the places that once nourished the minds, imagination, and souls of previous generations. Without much forethought or foresight we have designed a world convenient for commerce, speed, and violence, not one for children. As a consequence, most children grow up in the sterile world of freeways, concrete, steel, suburbs, shopping malls, television, iPods, and computer screens. The sum total of that is told in statistics about poverty, hunger, the spread of preventable disease, loneliness, and by the relentless numbers describing species loss, soil erosion, carbon in the atmosphere. Had we loved our children better, we would not have done so much so carelessly.

H. G. Wells once said that we are in a race between catastrophe on one side and education on the other. The dimensions of the possible catastrophe ahead are well documented. On the other side, there is a worldwide movement to remake the human presence on Earth by designing with, not against, nature. Ecological design involves the calibration of human intentions with the knowledge of how the world works as a physical system and the use of that knowledge to inform and discipline our intentions. It is rooted in the awareness of our proper role as members in the community of life and as players in the ongoing drama of evolution. It is predicated on the idea that nature is both a template and a model for human design, not something to be overwhelmed and mastered. The art and science of ecological design is rapidly changing how we build, farm, make, energize, transport, and dispose. When we get it right, it is from waste to life in an endless cycle.

Most important, ecological design—the practical application of the concepts of interrelatedness, systems, and long time horizons—is changing how we think, and how we think about the act of thinking. No improvement in our gadgetry and technology alone is remotely adequate to our situation without a profound change in our mindset. We arrived at our present precarious situation as a result of flaws in thinking, perception, and paradigm. That makes it a crisis for those who purport to improve such things, including, preeminently, educators, teachers, and the designers and builders of schools. Imagine, as Maria Montessori once did, schools without conceptual walls and barriers to imagination. Imagine schools powered entirely by sunlight that also purifies waste water that irrigates gardens that grow food and teach biology. Imagine schools as incubators for a new generation of designers that will remake the human presence on Earth in ways that regenerate ecologies and create the foundation for a fair, decent, and prosperous post-carbon economy. Imagine schools that foster the kind of thinking that bridges the chasms of ethnicity, nationality, religion, species, and time. Imagine a

world made sustainable because we first taught every child to overcome hatred and fear and educated them to be ecologically competent. Imagine schools that draw forth the very best from each child.

Bruce Mau, OWP/P, and VS Furniture exemplify the new generation of designers in what they have produced together. They have assembled the 79 ideas in this book as a blueprint for schools and education that could move the human prospect from catastrophe to the dawn of a far better future than what is in view. Nothing proposed here is impossible or farfetched; on the contrary, many are already applied in the best schools around the world. The concepts, ideas, and possibilities are practical but visionary, representing the core of a new Enlightenment that is spreading worldwide.

David W. Orr is currently professor and chair of the Environmental Studies Program at Oberlin College. He is perhaps best known for his pioneering work on environmental literacy in higher education and his recent work in ecological design. He spearheaded the effort to design and build the Environmental Studies Center at Oberlin College, a building described by the New York Times as "the most remarkable" of a new generation of college buildings and selected as one of 30 "milestone buildings" in the 20th century by the U.S. Department of Energy. David Orr is the author of four books, including The Nature of Design and The Campus and Environmental Responsibility.

THE COLLABORATORS

EDUCATION ARCHITECTS OWP/P, EDUCATION FURNITURE
DESIGNERS VS, AND DESIGN THINKERS BRUCE MAU DESIGN

Collaborative learning, according to experts on the subject, unleashes
a unique intellectual and social energy. We can attest to that. This book
is the result of a learning experience that began when three design firms
joined forces on an unprecedented project.

Education architects OWP/P had long had the desire to produce a book about the link between learning and environment. The moment OWP/P invited BMD, as design thinkers and book designers, and VS, as designers of furniture for the educational environment, to collaborate on such a book, there was a shift. The triumvirate took on the challenge and the idea took on substance.

Through a series of workshops in the United States, Canada, Germany, and England, we began to explore, together, what the book could and should be. We went on field trips, visiting classrooms, showrooms, conferences, even a factory floor—anywhere that would help us understand how design and the learning environment intersected. We read books and magazines. We watched videos and listened to podcasts. We combed through websites, journals, and archives. We spoke to students, teachers and parents; scientists, activists, and entrepreneurs; even a chef and a troubadour. The multiple perspectives multiplied our knowledge, ideas, and ambitions for this book exponentially.

Through it all, we collaborators talked with one another. We talked about what we saw, heard, read, and believed. We swapped horror stories and traded tales of hope. You'll find some of that discussion in the pages that follow, elaborating and commenting on the ideas inspired by the interviews, excerpts, and case studies that we eventually selected from our boxes and files of research. To work on this book was to become deeply engaged in the urgency and potential of this project. It became personal for each one of us, and we'd like you to hear our voices—because, more than anything, we'd like to hear your voices, as part of an international conversation about the power of the Third Teacher to transform teaching and learning. The end of this book is just the beginning—log on to thethirdteacher.com and join us for the next chapter.

WHY US?

There is a best-selling book called *Three Cups of Tea*. It's a memoir of humanitarian Greg Mortenson, who fell ill trying to climb K2 in the Himalayas. He was nursed back to health in the Pakistani village of Korphe, and was inspired to return the favor. He founded the Central Asia Institute, which nurtures community health by building village schools.

At OWP/P, we build schools in places less remote, but no less in need of community. There is a suburb of Chicago called Lincolnshire Village. Its first school opened in 1836 in a settler's home. One hundred and forty years later, Lincolnshire's population exploded, and its school—by then 800 students—needed to triple in size. We designed that expansion, and several more in the 20 years since, so that Lincolnshire could remain a village in spirit as well as in name.

When I think about what schools will be like in the decades to come, I imagine classrooms that are technology caves, where, for example, children in Lincolnshire are virtually in a room with children in Korphe. The two groups see each other, they converse and interact, even though they are thousands of miles apart. What I am imagining is not a place but a relationship, a relationship between cultures. As the world gets smaller, there is a growing urgency that we teach our children both to embrace identity and to navigate difference, not only with children down the block but also with children on the other side of the world. Our role as designers of schools is to understand what environmental characteristics support a collaborative approach to schooling. That is where learning occurs, and where communities—local and global—are built.

In our offices, we talk about these concepts all the time. When OWP/P was founded 50 years ago, our focus was youth education, and this focus continues to be a pillar of the firm. But to hold a conversa- tion about learning and environment solely within the confines of our practice is to limit the potential of that conversation to have global impact. Our commitment to the improvement of life through environments that are effective and inspiring and sustainable is the reason we initiated an international collaboration to create a book about environment and learning. A book is the most tangible and accessible of all communication tools and, to paraphrase the creativity and place-making expert Charles Landry, it takes our endeavor from being in the world to being for the world.

John M. Syvertsen

John Syvertsen, president, OWP/P

WHY THIS?

When my father was a boy, he used to play with Mario Montessori. Mario Montessori was the only son of Maria Montessori, the Italian doctor who reformed education with her belief that children do not learn by obeying rules and reproducing behavior, but by discovering and exercising their own strengths and abilities in an environment suited to that self-determination.

Shortly before World War I, Maria Montessori came to Berlin, where my grandfather, P. Johannes Müller, had founded a company making school furniture. My grandmother went to hear Maria Montessori's first lecture at Berlin University and, soon afterward, my grandfather became the sole producer of Montessori teaching aids for the German market. He and my grandmother became supporters of Maria Montessori's vision, and she was a frequent visitor at their home. She always traveled with her son and, even though Mario was five or six years older than my father, they would play together and Mario would instruct my father on how to use Montessori materials.

Mario went on to work with his mother on advancing the Montessori way, and my father went on to take over my grandfather's company, VS Furniture, of which I am now CEO. Today we manufacture a wide range of furniture for schools, guided by our conviction that the learning environment can bring the student and the teacher together into a relaxed and positive atmosphere for learning. According to Maria Montessori and her fellow Italian educator Loris Malaguzzi, whose writing inspired the title of this book, everything that is material affects the child's temperament and development. In a conducive environment, a child can learn many things without being taught in traditional ways.

In the early years of the 20th century, VS worked with a number of notable architects and designers, including members of the Bauhaus, on schools where the entire environment—from doors and windows to desks and lighting—was approached as a single project to support learning and development. But in later decades, the environmental, ergonomic, and pedagogical factors of school design were neglected in favor of the logistical, budgetary, and bureaucratic.

Enough time has passed for us to have seen what happens when we lose sight of the real project of schools. That is why we are ready to embrace again the vision that motivated my grandparents, the vision of schoolhouse and classroom as one material world centered on the child.

Thomas Müller

Dr. Thomas Müller, CEO, VS Furniture

WHY NOW?

When I was in school, having an *Encyclopaedia Britannica* was an important thing. You had to have it, all 32 volumes with their foil-stamped spines. Today we have Wikipedia, and we know how limited the old encyclopedias were, and how dated, almost immediately. For some time now, our technological capacity—our capacity to move information that shapes the world—has been doubling every year. That algorithm means that children starting kindergarten this fall will have, according to futurist Ray Kurzweil, a million times greater capacity to shape the world around them by the time they finish university.

And yet, schools still behave as though everything a child needs to know is on one piece of paper. Teachers tear little scraps off that piece of paper and hand them across a desk to the child, who eventually has the sum total of that one piece of paper. Well, today, the child has her own piece of paper. My eldest daughter is 14, and hers is full of information, even though she may not understand precisely how to structure it. At Bruce Mau Design we believe that everything communicates. A mall-sized school where learning consists of handing out scraps of paper in a classroom that is a quarter-mile away from fresh air: What does that communicate to a child about our understanding of, expectations about, and commitment to his future?

It is no surprise, then, that in the United States alone a third of all students drop out of school. A failure rate that high, in any enterprise, makes a systems collapse a very plausible scenario. However, it is not the only plausible scenario. At Bruce Mau Design, we are optimistic. That perspective allows us to see purpose and possibility in entirely new ways, and it produced our recent book and exhibition, *Massive Change*. For more than 20 years, in collaboration with some of the world's leading architects and institutions, artists and entrepreneurs, academics and businesses, we have been using design to take on important questions in an exchange that is open, inventive, and ultimately productive. Schools face one such important question: What is a great learning environment in the Wikipedia age? Now is the time to use design to take on that question. This book is the first step in an exchange we believe will provide answers.

Bruce Mau, chairman, Bruce Mau Design, Inc.

TABLE OF CONTENTS

1

BASIC NEEDS   24

Raffi: Honoring The Child / Basic Needs Come First / The Physiological Vulnerability of School Children / Indoor Air Quality as a Learning Opportunity / Perspectives on Indoor Air Quality / Guardians of the Indoor Environment / Strategies for Enhancing Wanted Sounds / Thomas Deacon Academy: Peterborough, England

2

MINDS AT WORK   50

Sir Ken Robinson: The Creativity Challenge / Neurological Growth Spurts / Right Brain, New Mind / Moving as Thinking / Howard Gardner: Smart Spaces for All Learners / Learning in Museums / Henry Ford Academy / Key Learning Community / Ministry of Education New High Schools: Cayman Islands

3

BODIES IN MOTION   76

Dr. Dieter Breithecker: The Body-Brain Connection / Perspectives Charter School / Engaged Learning / Invitation to Play / Hampden Gurney Church of England Primary School / Brains in Motion / Playgrounds and the War Against Obesity / Creating Playgrounds Kids Love / Fridtjof Nansen School: Hannover, Germany

WHAT WE LEARNED FROM STUDENTS AND PROFESSIONALS

Designers solve problems. Faced with complex challenges, the designer's job is to come up with solutions at every scale, from cities and systems to spoons and microchips. Those solutions must be delightful and functional, because great design is an innovative meld of both.

This book is full of solutions that feel right, work well, and look great, solutions drawn from relevant research, real schools—and from the people whose job it is to design and furnish those schools, as well as teach and learn in them. Teachers and learners made a critical contribution to this book because they helped us to understand their needs and challenges, dreams and hopes for their own learning environments. Designers call that information and insight "the user experience," and without a deep understanding of it there can be no truly delightful and functional design solution.

That's why we invited kids and their educators into the design process for this book. We asked them all kinds of questions: If you could design your ideal learning environment, what would it look like? How would it feel? Would it be open and collaborative as a studio, or small and snug as a cubby? What does the school of the future look like? How does it sit in its community, in its landscape, in the world?

We talked to students of various ages in three cities on two continents: a class of grade two and three students at Ogden Junior Public School in Toronto, Canada; a group of teenagers at Chicago Academy for the Arts in Chicago, United States; and two classes of 14- and 15-year-olds at Robert-Jungk Secondary School in Berlin, Germany.

Designers from BMD, OWP/P, and VS led each group of students in a pair of workshops that began with a presentation—a design primer to raise important questions, introduce key concepts, and establish a basic vocabulary. With that in hand, the students were sent off to reflect and collect images, words, drawings, and photos of designed elements and environments. During the second session, the students worked in small groups, matching material, that they had collected and we had provided, with school-day tasks, programs, and personal desires. Older kids were asked to consider the school in the context of the larger community and ecosystem. Younger kids were asked to connect activities with design elements that made them feel a certain emotion. The sessions were an open forum for students to voice their concerns, discuss and visualize their ideas, and speculate on their ideal learning environment.

As an epilogue to the student workshops, design and education professionals gathered in London, England, for a "design dinner." In that convivial environment they discussed the results of the student workshops, shared experiences, and rallied for change.

On the following pages, between chapters, we introduce those students and professionals and their ideas. We learned much from the workshops and we hope you will too. We hope you come away from this book inspired to work together—architects and clients, children and adults, students and lifelong learners—to radically transform the education landscape.

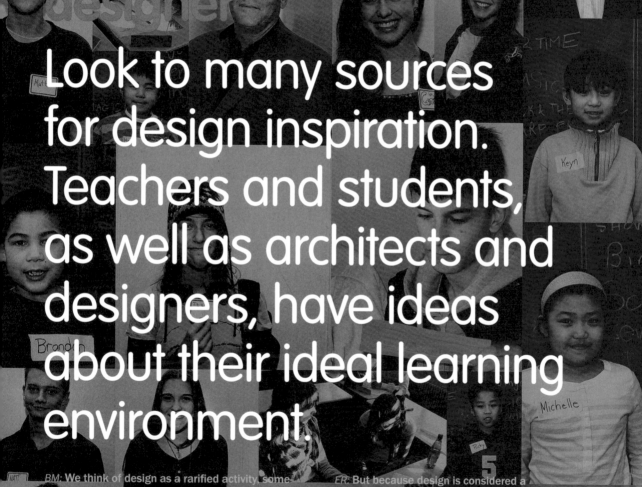

Everyone can be a designer

Look to many sources for design inspiration. Teachers and students, as well as architects and designers, have ideas about their ideal learning environment.

BM: We think of design as a rarified activity, something only designers do. But in fact, our language gives away how false that is. We use the word "design" quite intelligently, and we talk about designing things all the time—designing events, designing programs, designing solutions. Design methodology is actually more common than we realize.

ER: But because design is considered a foreign art, not a skill of everyday life, we don't teach it in schools, and we should.

—Bruce Mau and Elva Rubio, BMD

CHAPTER 1

BAS
NEL

It costs nearly three times more to provide health care for a child with asthma than a child without asthma. In 2006, this amount is equal to $1,650 per child. Note that most of these health costs are not borne by the schools, but rather by the students and their families.

Asthma is the most common chronic disorder in childhood, currently affecting an estimated 6.2 million children under 18 years of age.

A recent review by Carnegie Mellon of five separate studies evaluating the impact of improved indoor air quality on asthma found an average reduction of 38.5% in asthma in buildings with improved air quality.

American school children missed 12 million days of school in 2000 due to asthma.

The large majority of schools are built not to optimize health and comfort, but rather to achieve a minimum required level of design performance at the lowest cost. —Gregory Kats, principal, Capital E

Research indicates that high levels of background noise, much of it from heating and cooling systems, adversely affects learning environments, particularly for young children, who require optimal conditions for hearing and comprehension.

Sources (top to bottom): The Commonwealth of Massachusetts, *Attacking Asthma, Combating an epidemic among our children,* and Center for Disease Control, "Health, United States, 2005," in Capital E, *Greening America's Schools: Costs and Benefits;* Capital E, *Greening America's Schools: Costs and Benefits;* Carnegie Mellon University Center for Building Performance, in Capital E, *Greening America's Schools: Costs and Benefits;* American Federation of Teachers, *Building Minds, Minding Buildings: Turning Crumbling Schools into Environments for Learning;* Capital E, *Greening America's Schools: Costs and Benefits;* National Clearinghouse for Educational Facilities, *Do School Facilities Affect Academic Outcomes?*

The air is unfit to breathe in nearly 15,000 schools.

Students and faculty typically spend 85% to 90% of their time indoors (mostly at home and at school), and the concentration of pollutants indoors is typically higher than outdoors, sometimes by as much as 10 or even 100 times.

Students with limited classroom daylight were outperformed by those with the most natural light by 20% in math and 26% on reading tests.

Many classrooms feature a speech intelligibility rating of 75% or less. That means listeners with normal hearing can understand only 75% of the words read from a list.

14 million students (more than a quarter of all students) attend schools considered below standard or dangerous, and almost two-thirds of schools have building features such as air conditioning that are in need of extensive repair or replacement. This statistic does not include schools with less obvious but important health related-problems such as inadequate ventilation.

Sources (top to bottom): General Accounting Office Report # HEHS-95-95, "School Facilities: America's Schools not Designed or Equipped for the 21st Century," in Capital E, *Greening America's Schools: Costs and Benefits*; U.S. Environmental Protection Agency, "Indoor Air Quality"; National Clearinghouse for Educational Facilities, *Do School Facilities Affect Academic Outcomes?*; KI Education, "American School & University: Creating Positive, High Performance Learning Environments"; General Accounting Office Report # HEHS-95-95, "School Facilities: America's Schools not Designed or Equipped for the 21st Century," in Capital E, *Greening America's Schools: Costs and Benefits*

I am entirely certain
that 20 years from
now we will look
back at education
as it is practiced in
most schools today
and wonder how
we could have
tolerated anything
so primitive.

—John W. Gardner

John William Gardner, secretary of Health, Education, and Welfare under U.S. president Lyndon Johnson, wrote those words in *No Easy Victories*, his 1968 book on the challenges of social reform. His word for the schools of his day—"primitive"—was a daring one to throw out at a time when progress seemed unstoppable. However, in Gardner's America not only the education system but the schools themselves had become victims, rather than beneficiaries, of postwar prosperity. The baby boom had impelled mass production of huge new school buildings, constructed using low-cost building products, synthetic compounds created during the war, and standardized, mechanized systems.

We now know the hazards of many of those postwar materials and methods—the formaldehyde-soaked carpeting, the mercury-treated drywall, the sealed windows and noisy ventilation—but millions of school buildings containing those toxins and irritants are still in use, and children are expected to learn in aging structures that were never very safe or sound in the first place. "Primitive" remains the best word to describe many of today's learning environments.

This book starts with an examination of the basic needs of the child and the basic requirements of the child's learning environment because, unless those environments are safe and clean, it will be a challenge to achieve any learning and teaching that is itself more than primitive. Experts in child development and authorities on health and safety join teachers and designers in a heartfelt and fact-based plea for learning environments that address the fundamental necessities of life.

RAFFI
HONORING THE CHILD

Raffi Cavoukian is known to millions simply as Raffi. A generation grew up singing his classic, "Baby Beluga"; the renowned Canadian troubadour was once called "the most popular children's singer in the English-speaking world." A recipient of the Order of Canada and the United Nations' Environmental Achievement Award, Raffi is associated with many NGOs and has now become a "global troubadour," lecturing and networking to help create a viable future: a restorative, child-friendly world for ourselves and for those to come. He is the founder of Child Honouring, an integrated philosophy linking person, culture, and planet. Recently appointed a member of the Club of Budapest, Raffi makes the case that to do right by children, we must make schools—and all places children inhabit—healthy and safe.

You've evolved from a children's entertainer into a children's rights advocate. You're suggesting that we adopt the physicians' oath, "First, do no harm," as an approach to children. Why do we need that oath? A society that honors its young is one that has a chance of creating a humane, peacemaking, sustainable culture. If the young are not honored and respected for who they are, then they are going to grow up disenfranchised from their true authentic selves and are going to seek to connect in many, many afflicted ways.

Are you suggesting that, as a society, we currently are doing harm to children? Because we're not a child-honoring society, because children are not held in the kind of regard that they need to be held in, then I think we are, inadvertently, doing harm, yes. We don't even have a cultural understanding that it is not okay to physically punish children, that it is not acceptable. In some places it's still not against the law. That's just an example. "First, do

no harm" isn't just about physical punishment. It's quite broad. The "Covenant for Honouring" principles that I wrote, the nine child-honoring principles, all apply when we are thinking about how to design the optimal child-friendly learning space.

One of your principles is a "safe environment." How does that contribute to child honoring? Well, in the "safe environment" principle, the word "environment" doesn't just refer to air, water, and soil. We live in a number of environments. We live in a family environment, a learning environment, a work environment, the marketplace—that's an environment. You know the phrase "it takes a village to raise a child"? In the optimal village, in the "caring community," which is another child honoring principle, they are all safe environments.

Could you describe what a safe learning environment would be? I've listed the qualities that a school would want to evoke: that it would be fun

2.

Do no harm

Adopt this as an oath and a fundamental approach to children's learning environments.

and respectful; that it would inspire wonder; that it would enable creative play, individually and in groups. A school should engender a sense of community. There should be age-appropriate tools and resources. There should be a physical building that provides nurture and protection, especially in the early years. When I say "protection," it can even mean choosing what learning tools you don't bring in at too early an age—for example, the electronic

A society that honors its young is one that has a chance of creating a humane, peacemaking, sustainable culture.

screen. We live in such a video-dominated world, and there's a tremendous amount of evidence that electronic visuals at too young an age actually interfere with a child's image-making capacities.

You've made an intensive study of child development over your career. How can a healthy and safe environment encourage learning? Well, what are we learning about? We're learning about the world inside of us, the world of emotions and impulses, and we're learning about the world outside of us, not only our relationships with it, but the materials that we find ourselves around. What is this floor made of? If there is carpeting, is it made of organic materials, like wool, for example? What are the toys made of? What is the desk made of? The paper—how is it bleached? Is it done with hydrogen peroxide and therefore environmentally benign, or is it a chlorine-bleached paper that poisons our air and our water? The toxic chemicals in that process end up in our blood and in our flesh. You see, everything that the child is immersed in is a learning opportunity. It's not just what you're "teaching" in a given moment.

In the context of school, the concept of health and safety tends to be taken literally, in terms of keeping hazardous objects and materials and actions out of the school. You're arguing for a much broader kind of thinking. Yes, because the child is the most vulnerable player. Early childhood is the formative experience for a lifetime of behaviors and a lifetime of health effects. So what we're talking about is taking our natural impulse

to nurture a student and extending that in a conscious way to every aspect of the physical environment that that child is learning in. For example, the playground would be made of materials that don't include pressure-treated wood. We would have integrated pest control, so that it's a pesticide-free environment. We get the same result, but we do it naturally, we don't poison anything. Every child would vote for that. If we run a democratic learning environment, we need to take that into consideration. What would a child vote for? I can bet money that every child of reasoning age who understood the questions would vote for a non-toxic alternative, every single time.

Some of the actions you're talking about are ones that we just need to be smart about. Some of them, though, have costs attached to them. How can people who are fighting for these choices make the case to those who hold the purse strings? Monetary price is one thing, but, in what is called "full-cost pricing," if you factor in the cost of the social and environmental impacts of a product that you're bringing to market, you can't afford to bring a poisonous product to market. We can't knowingly sell a poisonous batch of milk in stores. Why, then, can we tolerate a world wherein the breast milk of mothers may contain residues of toxic chemicals that in a comparable volume of cow's milk would be banned from stores? There is a learning here about why we have to go a benign route. There is no real alternative to it. It's a no-brainer. We must not let the temporary greater monetary cost of doing the right thing cloud our vision. The long-term need compels us to do right by the child.

The nine guiding principles for honoring children as detailed at raffinews.com are:

- Respectful love
- Diversity
- Caring community
- Conscious parenting
- Emotional intelligence
- Nonviolence
- Safe environments
- Sustainability
- Ethical commerce

3.

Cherish children's spaces

It's a natural impulse to nurture our young— let that impulse extend to the places where young people learn.

BM: We claim to be committed to the safety and health of children—then we put them in a context where the chemical load is really heavy. It may be invisible, but we know it's there.

ER: I've seen a fossil-fuel power plant right next to a series of schools. And this plant was spewing out heavy metals, like mercury, at levels way above the allowable average of the EPA, right next to the schools. We need to be concerned not only with making the buildings, but also the urban environment around them.

—Bruce Mau and Elva Rubio, BMD

BASIC NEEDS COME FIRST
A CHILDREN'S RIGHTS ORGANIZATION CITES A PIONEER
OF PSYCHOLOGY TO EXPLAIN WHY LEARNING CAN'T
BEGIN UNTIL BASIC NEEDS ARE MET

Abraham Maslow (1908–1970) was one of the founders of humanistic psychology. He hypothesized that people were guided by their needs, and as soon as one need was satisfied, they would move on to the next. He also recognized that some needs took precedence over others. Maslow formulated the Hierarchy of Needs, marking five stages of human growth. He envisioned a ladder, beginning at the bottom with the basic need for sustenance and culminating with transcendence. The rungs of the hierarchy are physiological needs, safety and security needs, belonging needs, esteem needs, and, finally, self-actualization, the peak of human existence.

How does this theory apply to children? Like all living organisms, from the microscopic amoeba to the majestic blue whale, children have inherent needs. The fulfillment of those needs, by themselves or with the help of family and the community, leads to healthy development and a strong foundation for adulthood. Any deficiency in these needs can handicap a child, hindering her performance at home, at school, and in adult life.

The first level consists of the basic physiological needs. For a child, these needs are food, water, and sleep. Once the physiological needs have been addressed, the next level is the safety and security needs. Adults tend to only think of their safety needs in times of emergency, whereas children often have a constant worry about their safety and security. For a child, these needs can be equally important at home, at school, and in the neighborhood. Finally, when all other needs have been satisfied, the quest for self-actualization begins.

Adapted from: "Maslow's Hierarchy of Needs"

For more: www.investinginchildren.on.ca

5 Self-Actualization
Pursue Inner Talent,
Creativity, & Fulfillment

4 Self-Esteem
Achievement, Mastery,
Recognition, & Respect

3 Belonging/Love
Friends, Family, Spouse,
& Lover

2 Safety
Security, Stability,
& Freedom From Fear

1 Physiological
Food, Water, Shelter,
& Warmth

4.

Put safety before study

Children are ready to learn only when they're safe and secure, so address those needs before considering any other aspect of a child's environment.

MB: A friend of mine used to teach in a low-income neighborhood, and his role was much more that of a counselor than that of a teacher. It's important to remember that for some children, school might be a really safe place compared to their homes and neighborhoods.

ER: For kids like that, principals and teachers always say that Monday mornings and Friday afternoons are the worst times. On Mondays, the kids come from these unsafe environments into school freaked out. Often the teachers have to feed them and clean them up. Then on Fridays, the kids start freaking out because they have to go back into their unsafe environments. You would think that in contemporary big American cities this wouldn't happen. But it does. School becomes the place where kids can have a meal, and attention, and people they can talk to. It is a place of refuge.

—*Monica Bueno and Elva Rubio, BMD*

THE PHYSIOLOGICAL VULNERABILITY OF SCHOOL CHILDREN

THE MANY REASONS WHY A LEARNING ENVIRONMENT THAT FAILS TO MEET BASIC NEEDS IS RISKIER FOR CHILDREN THAN FOR ADULTS

Children's organs are still developing. Their immature brains and lungs are more vulnerable to permanent damage and chronic disease from toxins and particulates. Their immature immune systems may not detoxify poisons.

Children have higher metabolic rates than adults, and so breathe more air per pound of body weight than adults. They also tend to engage in more physical activity. This increases their exposure to air particulates.

Metals such as lead and mercury and gases such as radon settle close to the floor. Because they are shorter, children breathe air closer to the floor. They play on the floor. They rarely wash their hands before eating.

Listening and hearing are developmental skills. The ability to focus on speech does not mature until ages 13–15. To correctly interpret spoken words, children need to hear consonant sounds clearly. These sounds can be masked by equipment that hisses or rumbles louder than a loud whisper.

Children are less able to identify and avoid hazards.

Children have a limited ability to spot danger that is out of their direct line of sight. While adults have peripheral vision of 180 degrees, a child in first grade has peripheral vision of only 120 degrees. Up to the age of 10, a child's entire sensory system is undergoing critical development and isn't fully developed until the child is.

Adapted from: "Healthy and Safe School Environment, Part II, Physical School Environment", and Dr. D. Breithecker, head of the Federal Institute on the development of posture and exercise
For more: www.ashaweb.org

5.
Think small

When identifying hazards in the learning environment, remember that children are more physically vulnerable than adults.

There's another way we need to think small: We need to consider that a small amount of a harmful substance can have a big effect, particularly on a developing system. We used to think that unless we had significant exposure to a toxin we were okay, but what's surprising scientists is the discovery that we are vulnerable to even a very small amount or very low concentration of a harmful substance— it can act like a hormone and trigger results in the body that are out of proportion.
—Bruce Mau, BMD

INDOOR AIR QUALITY AS A LEARNING OPPORTUNITY
A CANADIAN REPORT TELLS THE STORY OF A TEACHER WHO MADE A HEALTHY SCHOOL NOT ONLY A GOAL BUT A LESSON PLAN

The U.S. Environmental Protection Agency has produced a kit called "Tools for Schools." This is how one school in Nova Scotia, a province on Canada's East Coast, implemented elements of the kit.

The school, located in an economically depressed area of the province, was in a state of crisis about its heating and air circulation problems. Some school rooms were too hot while others were too cold, and school occupants were reporting headaches, tiredness, sore eyes, and asthma attacks. At the initiative of the chemistry teacher, students became involved in a year-long project to monitor the indoor environment. They learned how to take temperature readings throughout the school and, based on those, were able to make some small, immediate changes. Then, they held a presentation on "Tools for Schools" and distributed its checklists to staff. The lists were returned to the students, who, with the help of the teacher and maintenance staff, tabulated the results and prioritized the issues. The students made Indoor Air Quality, or IAQ, the topic of their science fair, which informed the community about the initiative and initial improvements. By year end, the number of annual IAQ complaints at the school had dropped from 1,000 to 10. **Adapted from:** *Indoor Air Quality in Canadian Schools: Final Report* **For more:** www.ahprc.dal.ca

PERSPECTIVES ON INDOOR AIR QUALITY
A PARENT, A STUDENT, AND A SUPERVISOR SPEAK OUT ON THE REASONS A SCHOOL'S INDOOR AIR QUALITY MATTERS

"As parents of children with asthma, we work hard to prevent asthma attacks. But what about when they go to school? The school community can take an active role in improving Indoor Air Quality." —*parent, Tennessee*

"I have seen firsthand the ripple effect it has when a young person encourages participation and good habits concerning indoor air quality. It may seem strange to see a young person sincerely pursue a technical, typically adult issue, but who better to get involved than the youth. We have creative potential; it only has to be inspired." —*student, Washington*

"Staying proactive on IAQ issues not only helps our students achieve, it also helps us avoid distractions, liability headaches, and public relations worries. By involving parents and the community in IAQ prevention, we have avoided confrontations over minor problems and stayed focused on the classroom."

—*retired superintendent, Illinois*

Adapted from: "Actions to Improve Indoor Air Quality"

For more: www.epa.gov

6.

Assign the solution

Make health and safety a classroom project and develop lesson plans that will produce real improvements to the learning environment.

HS: Every province and state has a set curriculum with standards and expectations that are legislated. Teachers have to cover the curriculum—as well as prepare students for standardized tests. It takes a lot of time, initiative, and enthusiasm to integrate add-ons into an already packed curriculum. Most teachers would like to, but it depends on variables such as how many students they have in their classes, whether those students have special needs, and what those needs are. The reality is that sometimes it's just not possible.

TL: We know that there are educators out there who develop an entirely project-based pedagogy, who are integrating core subjects into projects rather than teaching to tests.

—*Helen Hirsh Spence, educational consultant to VS Furniture, and Trung Le, OWP/P*

GUARDIANS OF THE INDOOR ENVIRONMENT

THE NATIONAL EDUCATION ASSOCIATION DRAWS A DIRECT LINK BETWEEN HOW SCHOOLS ARE CLEANED AND HOW STUDENTS FEEL

While the indoor environment of schools is everyone's responsibility, many look to education support professionals—most especially custodial and maintenance staff—as the guardians of the indoor environment. They must have access to the necessary information, tools, techniques, and management systems to achieve healthy conditions. The best available cleaning technology, supplies, and professional development should be provided to school custodians. Effective cleaning equipment and an organized cleaning program that emphasizes the correct use of equipment will provide for an environment where all members of the school community can perform at their best. **Adapted from:** *Take a Deep Breath and Thank Your Custodian*

For more: www.neahin.org

Protect human health.
Choose cleaning products that:

Have no short-term (acute) or long-term (chronic) health hazards

Use disinfectants only as required by state health laws

Contain no known, probable, or possible carcinogens

Are non-irritating to eyes & skin

Are free of, or are low in, Volatile Organic Compounds (VOCs)

Avoid fragrances (odors) and dyes

Have neutral pH

7.

Make janitors guardians

School custodians and caretakers play a vital role in protecting student health. Respect that role by providing cleaning staff with the best available training, technology, and supplies.

The European model for custodians is that they live on-site. At one school that our colleague, Kerry Leonard, visited in the United Kingdom, the custodian happened to love chess. He was taking care of the school, and he was also teaching the kids how to play chess. The school was turning out national chess champions. This one person, this custodian, was changing kids' lives.

—Trung Le, OWP/P

STRATEGIES FOR ENHANCING WANTED SOUNDS

THE NOISE POLLUTION CLEARINGHOUSE EXPLAINS WHY CLASSROOM ACOUSTICS ARE CRUCIAL TO LEARNING AND HOW THEY CAN BE IMPROVED

Studies of speech recognition confirm that an adult listener hearing words in the context of a sentence can fill in words or syllables that are not heard clearly. Since children have smaller vocabularies, they are less able to fill in the words not heard clearly. Similarly, someone using English as a second language, or someone who suffers from an attention deficit disorder, is at a significant disadvantage in a noisy classroom. In addition, many children with usually normal hearing have temporary hearing losses from illness. Otitis media, a bacterial infection of the middle ear, is the most frequently occurring childhood medical complaint.

Adapted from: "Classroom Design for Good Hearing"

For more: www.quietclassrooms.org

Requirements for good hearing in the classroom:
- A quiet background (i.e., no noise from intruding traffic, adjacent classes, ventilation systems, etc.)
- Control of reverberation and self-noise

To control unwanted sounds:
- Locate schools away from highways, rail tracks, and flight paths
- Minimize noise intrusion from outdoors
- Minimize interference between classrooms
- Design quiet ventilation system

Ceiling: Acoustical ceiling tile with noise reducing co-efficient of .70 or higher

Top of Walls: Surface-mounted fabric-wrapped panels with either a sound-absorbent or sound-diffusive core

Furnishings: Some soft furniture to absorb sound

Front Walls: Hard wall surfaces to reflect sound to the rear of the classroom

Floor: Sound-absorbing material such as carpeting

Rear Walls: Surface-mounted fabric-wrapped panels with sound-absorbent core

8.

Design for speech and hearing

Acoustics isn't just for concert halls: Using sound-absorbent materials in classrooms is a simple and effective way to ensure that teachers can focus on teaching, not repeating.

CR: **This makes the perfect case for soft furnishings in school, because they become part of the acoustic solution. Not everything in a school has to have a hard surface.**

RD: **As learning spaces evolve into more open environments, we're going to have to pay more attention to acoustical engineering. We're starting to see the complexity of this issue.**

TL: **There's a common belief that learning environments need absolute quiet. That isn't necessarily true. If learners are really engaged in their work, they'll feel connected and energized by a certain amount of noise, not distracted.**

—Claudius Reckord, VS Furniture, Rick Dewar and Trung Le, OWP/P

THOMAS DEACON ACADEMY
PETERBOROUGH, ENGLAND

The Thomas Deacon Academy, designed by Foster + Partners, is an innovative new learning environment that reinvents the traditional school model. The building comprises two ribbons of classrooms that enclose a central concourse sheltered beneath a dramatic, light- transmitting roof. The curves of the perimeter classrooms create six distinct three-story colleges, each containing teaching areas and communal spaces. This arrangement breaks down the scale of the building, both physically and socially, and by increasing the external edge maximises the potential to draw natural light and ventilation inside.

Thomas Deacon Academy was built under the United Kingdom's Building Schools for the Future (BSF) government program. BSF represents a new approach to capital investment. It is bringing together significant investment in buildings and in ICT (Information and Communications Technology) over the coming years to support the government's educational reform agenda. BSF aims to ensure that secondary pupils learn in 21st-century facilities. By 2011, every local authority in England will have received funding to renew at least the school in greatest need. By 2016, major rebuilding and remodeling projects (at least three schools) will have started in every local authority.

— "About BSF: Better Secondary School Buildings to Support Educational Reform" www.teachernet.gov.uk

Natural daylight improves the working environment, and has been shown to increase concentration and learning. Daylight can also have an uplifting effect on feelings of well-being and health. It is important for the inhabitants of the building to be aware of the outside environment as it changes throughout the school day. The idea was that no classroom would directly overlook another part of the building—the classrooms are angled so that almost every one provides an open aspect, with views of the surrounding mature trees. The angles of the six "v"-shaped wings of the building were carefully considered to maximize the daylight that enters the rooms. In the "pinch points" between the wings where natural daylight would be minimal, we located utilitarian parts of the building—escape stair cores, toilet blocks, and service risers. Positioning the teaching wall perpendicular to the window wall minimizes glare and distraction yet provides plenty of natural light. The glazed partitions between the teaching spaces and central concourse area provide a secondary source of natural light, borrowed from the undulating central concourse roof.

The students, staff, and visitors are in awe of the roof. There is a noticeable sense of pride in the pupils; some seem to have found a new enthusiasm for attending school. Indeed, one young girl told us that whereas she used to dread Monday morning and the week ahead, now she really looks forward to coming to school every day. It is important for pupils to understand that their education is important enough to deserve such an unusual and special building. The waves and swells of the concourse roof successfully knit together the individual colleges, creating a building that is awe inspiring yet not intimidating. The flood of natural daylight creates a central space that is fantastic to spend time in. It also minimizes the use of electric lights, which means that energy can be saved. It is vital that children gain knowledge of the importance of conserving energy and saving the planet.

Many of the study spaces and the main library/resource centre are situated directly beneath the undulating concourse roof. Combining that with the fact that these spaces are surrounded by circulation, where students typically 'let off steam' when moving between lessons, means that acoustics were critical in this central space. All roof panels that are not glazed are acoustic panels, the outer faces of the balustrades are finished in an acoustic render, and the carpeted floor also contributes to the acoustic success of the central space.

The majority of the teaching spaces are naturally ventilated. The low level windows are manually operated, allowing the inhabitants of the room to open and close the windows as they please. The top windows can be automatically controlled to open the high level vents in the evening to allow night-time cooling. **Adapted from:** "Thomas Deacon Academy opens for the new school year"; Eleanor Baxter, interview with Angelica Fox, BMD
For more: www.fosterandpartners.com

9.

Let the sunshine in

And the gray skies too: Increasing daylight in classrooms has been shown to cut down on absenteeism and improve test scores.

ER: Most of our schools were built in the late 1950s through the 1970s. Those buildings are a certain way because of the invention of air-conditioning, and also because of the political mood of the era when they were built. In the United States, it was during the civil rights movement, and there was a lot of violence. Buildings were turning inward, literally, and blocking out the world because it was so bad. What we're seeing are leftovers of that time.

TL: I think cost may have been an even greater influence than social unrest on school design of the 1960s and 70s. Back then, they were designing with limited resources, and glass was expensive. They were also trying to limit learning distraction and conserve energy.

—*Elva Rubio, BMD and Trung Le, OWP/P*

WHAT WE LEARNED AT:
OGDEN JUNIOR PUBLIC SCHOOL
TORONTO, CANADA
THE STUDENTS TELL US WHAT THEY LIKE TO DO AND
WHERE THEY LIKE TO DO IT

"Play is fun. Sometimes work is
more important, but playing keeps
you active."

"I'd like to write a story on a big,
big rock—where it's quiet and
I can concentrate."

"We only use our tables and chairs
when we're doing our work. We use
the carpet for Show and Tell and
Listening—that's so we can hear
better and see the pictures clearly."

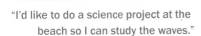

"I'd like to do a science project at the
beach so I can study the waves."

"I'd like to write a story while I'm at
a museum, because there are a lot of
interesting things to write about."

10.

Shuffle the deck

Change up the locations of regular activities so children can explore new surroundings with their bodies and their minds.

CHAPTER 2

MINI
AT W

The true purpose of education is to make minds, not careers. —William Deresiewicz, literary critic

Victorian schools were designed to meet the particular needs of the Victorian era. They were created to turn out "obedient specialists": adults who could work in factories, assembling components, or as domestic servants, not people who needed to think for themselves.

—Sean McDougall, educational thinker and designer

Students who are not exposed to arts and music in school score lower on standardized tests and have worse communication skills than those who do.

A central challenge for the education system is to find ways of embedding learning in a range of meaningful contexts where students can use their knowledge and skills creatively to make an impact on the world around them. —Kimberly Seltzer, author and Tom Bentley, author and policy analyst

86% of voters believe that encouraging children to be creative and develop their imagination is necessary to maintain our competitive edge and ensure that we do not fall behind other countries.

Education must shift from instruction to discovery—to probing and exploration...

—Marshall McLuhan, educator and communications theorist

Sources (top to bottom): *The American Scholar,* "The Disadvantages of an Elite Education"; Futurelab, "The School of the Future"; Office of the Governor of the State of California, "Record Investment in Music, Arts & PE"; Kimberly Seltzer and Tom Bentley, *The Creative Age: Knowledge and Skills for the New Economy*; The Imagine Nation and Lake Research Partners, *The Imagine Nation Poll*; Marshall McLuhan, *The Medium Is the Massage*

Logic will get you from A to B. Imagination will take you everywhere.

—Albert Einstein, theoretical physicist

By 2014, according to our estimates, the U.S. will add another 10 million creative sector jobs to the nation's economy. The same pattern holds for virtually all of the advanced nations, where the creative class makes up 35% to 45% of the workforce, depending on the country.

The mind is not a vessel to be filled but a fire to be kindled.
—Plutarch, Greek historian and biographer

If you create a system where initiative and creativity is valued and rewarded, then you'll get change from the bottom up.

—Paul Pastorek, superintendent

In the U.S., the nonprofit arts and culture industry generates $166.2 billion in economic activity every year—$63.1 billion in spending by organizations and an additional $103.1 billion in event-related spending by their audiences.

It is the tension between creativity and skepticism that has produced the stunning and unexpected findings in science. —Carl Sagan, astronomer and author

Sources (top to bottom): World of Quotes, "Imagination"; Richard Florida, *Who's Your City?*; *Creating Minds*, "Creative quotes and quotations: On the Mind"; *The New York Times Magazine*, "A Teachable Moment"; Americans for the Arts, *Arts & Economic Prosperity III: The Economic Impact of Nonprofit Arts and Culture Organizations and Their Audiences*; Wisdom Quotes, "Carl Sagan"

The principal goal of education is to create men who are capable of doing new things, not simply repeating what other generations have done—men who are creative, inventive, and discoverers.

—Jean Piaget

Five months after the first humans landed on the moon, *Time* magazine ran that quote in a feature article on Jean Piaget, the then 73-year-old Swiss philosopher and child psychologist. The occasion was ostensibly what *Time* called "a flood" of Piaget translations pouring into the American market, but the world was clearly ready for Piaget's advice about educating discoverers. "His insights," said *Time*, "are in growing vogue among U.S. educators, psychologists and some parents...His findings have given encouragement and innumerable specific suggestions to the 'discovery method' of teaching, now used in many schools across the U.S. and in Great Britain."

A tour today of schools across the United States, Great Britain, and in fact most of the developed world would find little evidence of Piaget's philosophy in action. Creativity is ghettoized, restricted to a single period or a couple of shabby rooms. The tools and tactics that encourage the creative thinking that is now, more than ever, so critical to success in higher education and the world at large have yet to be integrated into the standard curriculum or overall design of our schools.

In this chapter, a chorus of voices echo Piaget, each making their own point in support of his pioneering observations about the goal of education. Creativity expert Ken Robinson says that all subjects should be given equal weight, and comparable facilities. Leading psychologist Howard Gardner is a vocal proponent of education that embraces multiple intelligences and appeals to the diverse learning styles and intellects of our children. We hear from creative and courageous teachers who have turned theory into practice, gaining knowledge from the museum model of self-directed, interpretative learning—configuring their classrooms to stimulate active collaboration. They are employing lessons from the Third Teacher in their classrooms every day, and it is time to support them systemically, in the design of both education and schools. We must give children spaces and lessons that foster lifelong creativity, that teach them to take calculated risks, to innovate and experiment. What does the future have in store? Only the creative mind can speculate.

SIR KEN ROBINSON
THE CREATIVITY CHALLENGE

Sir Ken Robinson is an internationally recognized leader in the development of creativity, innovation, and human resources. Now based in Los Angeles, he has worked with national governments in Europe and Asia, with international agencies, Fortune 500 companies, not-for-profit corporations, and some of the world's leading cultural organizations. He is the author of several influential papers and books, including his 1998 report for the U.K. government, *All Our Futures: Creativity, Culture, and Education*, and his latest book, *The Element: A New View of Human Capacity*. He argues that to meet the challenges ahead, we must redesign schools to nurture the creativity capacity in all of us.

You've pointed out that schools, as we know them, were designed at a particular time for a particular purpose. Can you talk about that? Well, the whole process of public education came about primarily to meet the needs of the Industrial Revolution in the 18th and 19th centuries, and the current system doesn't just represent the interests of the industrial model, it embodies them. To begin with, there's a very strong sense of conformity. Second, the pedagogical model is based on the idea of transmission. Teachers teach and students learn. That's buttressed by the idea that the efficient way to do this is to educate kids by age—as though the most important thing they have in common is their date of manufacture. And the third big feature is the hierarchy of subjects: You have science and math at the top, and languages, then the arts further down.

The school buildings represent all of that. You have separate facilities for different subjects. The classroom arrangements are people sitting facing the front where someone's speaking to them. And there are large examination rooms. It's the factory model.

You've been a professor, an author, a consultant, but you've said you were first struck by this as a teenager. What were you going through then? Much as I liked aspects of school, there were things I'd really have liked to do that I didn't get an opportunity to do. I never did music at school—it wasn't available for kids on my track. I wanted to do art but I couldn't because it clashed with other subjects people thought were more important. It was only when I was 16 that we managed to talk one of our teachers into putting some plays on. And that, to me, opened up a whole other door, a process of working with people differently from conventional academic work.

So I went off and did an English and theater degree, and trained as a teacher. The practice of the arts was thought to have lower status than academic work. And I never understood why that was, because it seemed to me that doing art is as complicated as doing art history; writing novels is a good bit more difficult than writing about them.

11.

Make it new

Look at your learning space with 21st-century eyes: Does it work for what we know about learning today, or just for what we knew about learning in the past?

MW: There's a values-based aspect to this discussion. It has to do with the way we see people and the way we think people should be treated. The industrial revolution model of education was actually very successful. It churned out carbon-copy mentalities at a time when society prized conformity. As we start to prize creativity instead, we need to look at how creativity can be fostered, and developed, and encouraged. There are technical and physical aspects to that, but also emotional and values-based ones.

TL: If we truly believe that creativity is an essential ingredient in a child's development, then we need to shift completely away from the "cells and bells" model of school design. So the other fundamental question we should be asking is: Does this learning environment support a child's natural instinct to learn through creation and discovery?

—*Michael Waldin, BMD and Trung Le, OWP/P*

So I got very interested in promoting drama in schools, and then it struck me that people who were promoting drama in schools were doing it in exactly the same way as people who were pushing for art and music in schools, but they never talked to one another about it. So I ended up running a big project in the U.K. called "The Arts in Schools." Lately, I've been looking at more creative approaches to science, and technology, and the humanities, and so on.

How would you respond to people who say to a story like yours, "You clearly turned out all right, despite the fact that you weren't allowed to study the arts initially. So why do we have to change education?" I'm always very hesitant when people say, "Well, it didn't do me any harm." I wish I could feel that confident. Of course it's true that some people get through. But what you can't take stock of are the countless people who didn't. In California, the state government last year spent $3.5 billion

If we're looking for new pedagogical practices, we have to have facilities that will enable those to happen.

on the state university system. In the same year, it spent nearly $9 billion on the state prison system. I cannot believe that more potential criminals are born every year in California than potential college graduates. So you can point to great musicians, and great writers—they made it, yes. But an awful lot of them made it in spite of the system, not because of it. If we were to think of the system differently, how many more would flower and flourish? How much better would that make all of our circumstances, rather than having so many people being at odds with one another in fundamental ways, because they're at odds with themselves?

You're calling for a redefinition of "back to basics," for thinking of creativity as one of the basics. The issue here is that a lot of people talk about getting back to basics, but they're basing this argument on the old economy. The future economies, and the present economy, absolutely depend on innovation and creativity. When I talk about getting back to basics I mean let's decide what we

need to do next. To me, number one is that the hierarchy has to go. There has to be equal weight given to the arts, the sciences, humanities, technology, and physical education. And therefore the facilities in which people are learning have to give equal provision to these activities. If it appears that some activities are more cherished because the facilities are grander, it sends a very powerful message to people about what matters. The physical environment of the building is critically important in terms of the curriculum.

The second thing is that real innovation and creativity come at the intersections of disciplines—the way they merge and blend. So you'd also want school buildings that allowed a permeability of practices, that allowed people across disciplines to work collaboratively. And the third thing, for me, is that, if we're looking for new pedagogical practices, we have to have facilities that will enable those to happen. So you want flexible spaces where people can group and re-group, where you're not stuck in one configuration with teachers at the front. The physical environment of the building is very important, but what really makes an institution is the habits of mind that become taken for granted in the community that occupies the institution. An institution is the people and their ways of thinking. If you really want to shift a culture, it's two things: its habits and its habitats—the habits of mind, and the physical environment in which people operate.

12.

Support great teaching

Free teachers from the traditional desk at the front of the classroom and encourage new settings for teaching and learning.

HS: As a school principal, I would have loved to have been able to provide collaborative time for my teachers to work together across disciplines. It would have made the most significant positive difference to learning, and to the whole school environment. I never had the freedom or the ability to do it—my timetabling was governed by other factors, such as union rules, staffing considerations, space. But, ideally, in planning a new school you could design for this kind of collaboration to take place much more naturally.

AH: In Germany, many teachers don't feel they have a great workplace to go to. We need to give them a professional working environment, so they feel they have a place where they can be creative, somewhere they can concentrate and prepare for their next class. If you're always stuck having to be in a classroom, you are missing opportunities for collaboration.

RD: Most of today's classrooms are designed with the teacher at the center. But if the classroom is focused on the learner instead, then learning becomes paramount.

—*Helen Hirsh Spence, educational consultant to VS Furniture; Dr. Axel Haberer, VS Furniture; and Rick Dewar, OWPP*

NEUROLOGICAL GROWTH SPURTS

AN EXPERT ON COGNITIVE DEVELOPMENT DELIVERS
EVIDENCE THAT STRONG MINDS ARE BUILT WITH
ONGOING CREATIVE CHALLENGES AND MENTORING

RIGHT BRAIN, NEW MIND

A PROFESSOR OF EDUCATION LAYS OUT THE
NEUROLOGICAL BASIS OF YOUNG PEOPLE'S NEED
FOR CREATIVE EXPLORATION

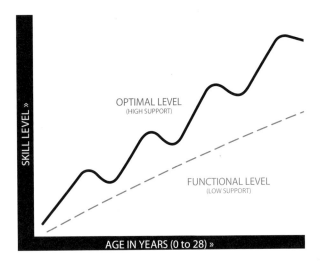

OPTIMAL LEVEL
(HIGH SUPPORT)

FUNCTIONAL LEVEL
(LOW SUPPORT)

SKILL LEVEL »

AGE IN YEARS (0 to 28) »

What does it mean for the brain to go through a growth cycle? Consider the brain's outer layers, known as the cortex. The cortex supports reasoning and thinking skills through its massive network of connections with the rest of the brain. Whenever neurons fire, a small amount of electrical energy is released. The amount of electrical activity in the cortex shows periodic spurts. These spurts occur at the same time as new skills emerge, say in musical performance or spatial reasoning. The spurts of electrical activity and attendant growth in connections support a new level of development. Just as physical growth shows dramatic spurts, learning also jumps in fits and starts. A child doesn't learn skills and concepts just once—he or she relearns them at successively more mature levels. But cognitive spurts only show up when children enjoy optimal learning conditions, such as the support of a good teacher or mentor. The figure above shows how students' ability to think abstractly differs, depending on whether support is available.

Adapted from: "What's the Brain Got to do with it?"

For more: www.uknow.gse.harvard.edu

The cerebrum at the top of our brain processes conscious thought and behavior. The sensory lobes at the back recognize and interpret current challenges, and the frontal lobes determine and execute an appropriate response. The role of the right and left hemispheres has been somewhat of an enigma.

Elkhonon Goldberg, writing in *The Wisdom Paradox* in 2005, suggests that the major question a brain must ask whenever it confronts a challenge is "Have I confronted this problem before?" He argues that, in most people, the right hemisphere lobes process novel challenges and develop creative solutions, and the left hemisphere lobes process familiar challenges and execute established routines.

Childhood and adolescence are characterized by many novel challenges, and so the right hemisphere in young people is more robust. As we age, we develop an increasingly large repertoire of routines that we incorporate into the resolution of a wide variety of challenges. Although both hemispheres activate whenever we confront a challenge, the left hemisphere assumes a greater role and becomes more robust as we age. It takes a lot of energy to understand and respond to novel challenges, so we tend to use responses we've already developed. We get set in our ways.

Schools are run by older people who know the answers, and the students are young people who want to explore the challenges. Schools thus often teach students the answers to questions they haven't yet asked, that don't engage them emotionally. Students obviously need to master basic skills and their cultural heritage, but the challenge for educators is to create the right mix of didactic instruction and creative student exploration—and to reflect this mix in standards and assessment programs. **Adapted from:** "Cognitive Neuroscience Discoveries and Educational Practices" **For more:** www.aasa.org

13.

Build neural networks

Spark cognitive development by providing students of all ages with places to test new skills.

This applies to lifelong learning. Learning is building neural pathways, and the capacity to grow the brain doesn't stop—you can expand your neural capacity at any age. That's why it's so important to continue to do challenging things as you age.

—Bruce Mau, BMD

MOVING AS THINKING
CREATIVITY EXPERT KEN ROBINSON SHARES THE STORY
OF HOW AN ACCLAIMED CHOREOGRAPHER ALMOST
MISSED HER CALLING

I'm doing a new book on how people discovered their talent. It's prompted by a conversation I had with a wonderful woman called Gillian Lynne. She's a choreographer: She did *Cats*, and *Phantom of the Opera*. Gillian and I had lunch one day and I said, "Gillian, how'd you get to be a dancer?" And she said it was interesting; when she was at school, she was really hopeless. And the school wrote her parents and said, "We think Gillian has a learning disorder." She couldn't concentrate, she was fidgeting. I think now they'd say she had ADHD.

She went to see this specialist, in this oak-paneled room. She was there with her mother, and she sat on her hands for 20 minutes while her mother talked about all the problems Gillian was having at school: she was disturbing people, her homework was always late, and so on. In the end, the doctor said, "Gillian, I've listened to all these things that your mother's told me, and I need to speak to her privately. Wait here, we'll be back, we won't be very long."

As they went out, the doctor turned on the radio that was sitting on his desk, and when they got out of the room, he said to Gillian's mother, "Just stand and watch her." And the minute they left the room, Gillian said, she was on her feet, moving to the music. And they watched for a few minutes and the doctor turned to her mother and said, "Mrs. Lynne, Gillian isn't sick; she's a dancer. Take her to a dance school."

I said, "What happened?" Gillian said, "She did. I can't tell you how wonderful it was. We walked in this room and it was full of people like me, people who couldn't sit still. People who had to move to think." **Adapted from:** *Sir Ken Robinson: Do schools kill creativity?* **For more:** www.TED.com

14.

Multiply intelligences

Allow students time and space to choose what they want to do—their choices will illuminate their individual strengths.

HS: Sometimes, it is still appropriate for students to sit in rows listening to their teachers talk from the front of a classroom. But being the "sage on the stage" is only one way to teach. Brain research is giving us great insights into how we can vary teaching methods to meet the needs of different learning styles. Good lessons need exquisite design—so that teachers can stretch students in their dominant and preferred learning styles, and also in their non-dominant styles. And of course good lessons also get students to access their right- and left-brain hemispheres.

RD: Howard Gardner's Multiple Intelligences Theory is implicitly asking the designer of the learning environment to consider a variety of learning spaces—spaces in diverse sizes, materials, and colors, as well as spaces with different transparency, connectivity, and agility. The one-size-fits-all idea really isn't acceptable any more.

—*Helen Hirsh Spence, educational consultant to VS Furniture and Rick Dewar, OWP/P*

HOWARD GARDNER
SMART SPACES FOR ALL LEARNERS

Howard Gardner is professor of cognition and education at the Harvard Graduate School of Education. In 2005, he was selected by *Foreign Policy* and *Prospect* magazines as one of 100 most influential public intellectuals in the world. The author of more than 20 books and several hundred articles, Gardner is best known for his Theory of Multiple Intelligences, a critique of the notion that there exists but a single human intelligence that can be assessed by standard psychometric instruments.

On the implications for learning environments of Multiple Intelligences Theory:

It is important that those ideas, concepts, theories that are worth teaching and understanding be presented in lots of different ways. By doing so, one arouses the various intelligences of young people and also reaches more students. And so, in addition to the traditional schools that prioritize linguistic and logical intelligence, learning environments should allow students to exercise their musical, spatial, bodily, naturalist, interpersonal, and intrapersonal intelligences. The actual materials, or layout of the spaces, are less important than the provision of ample opportunity to use these intelligences. So, for example, one need not devote extra space to encourage the use of spatial intelligences; rather one should make imaginative pedagogical use of the spatial arrays that are available—large, small, 2D, 3D, material, virtual, etc.

On what schools would look like if we took seriously the fact that there are differences between children:

School would be far more individualized than ever before. In the past, only the wealthy had personalized education. They could hire individual tutors and they could travel wherever they wanted to (though we can do it faster these days!). To start with, each child would have his own computer (laptop, desktop, whatever) and would be able to learn ideas and materials in ways that are comfortable for that child.

Young people would also be able to keep their own records of what's been learned, what's been produced, critiqued, etc. Some of these materials would be stored digitally, but it is also important to display scientific, artistic, and historic works that have been fashioned by students and teachers. In that way, I think that schools in the future are more likely to resemble children's museums or exploratoria.

In this context, I call your attention to the Explorama, part of the remarkable Danfoss Universe in Sonderborg, Denmark. This theme park is the best venue that I've seen for observing the various intelligences at work.

The Explorama features dozens of games, exercises, and challenges that draw on different intelligences or combinations of intelligences. These exhibits can be used by children as well as adults of all ages. While the Explorama is not a formal learning environment, individuals can learn a great deal about their own profile of intelligences at the site.

On what learning will be like in future:

Much of learning going forward will occur virtually, at all hours of the day and night, rather than in classrooms from 8–3:30. Also, the role of media centers, and the teaching of capacities needed for effective expression in the new digital media, will continue to increase. **Adapted from:** Interview with Angelica Fox, BMD, and "Why Multiple Intelligences Theory Continues to Thrive" **For more:** www.dpu.dk

15.

Display learning

Posting student work, both current and past, up on the walls tracks progress in a visible way.

BM: One of the challenges of moving so much intelligence onto computers is that you can't see the work. At the BMD studios, one of the ways we've combated that is with a very simple display technique. People in the studio knew that if they wanted to get my attention, what they had to do was put the work where I could see it as I was walking by. So now we tack our work up on four-foot by eight-foot foam-core boards and see how it evolves. Bill Buxton, who used to be chief scientist at Alias, spent some time with us in the studio, and when he went to Microsoft Research to become principal researcher, he said to them, "I need a box of four-by-eight foam core to use for display." They said, "We don't have the budget for it." He said, "If I wanted a computer, you'd order it, but I'll buy the foam core myself." One day he passed by a meeting that was going on, and it was clear it was getting bogged down. He quietly slipped in a couple of boards. Now they are standard issue at Microsoft.

TL: We're seeing the things kids are producing, and they aren't just two-dimensional and static anymore. This new generation is creating films and multimedia productions. With technology getting less and less expensive, multimedia presentation display is affordable—and essential.

—*Bruce Mau, BMD and Trung Le, OWP/P*

LEARNING IN MUSEUMS
A PROFESSOR OF ARTS IN EDUCATION ADVISES
SCHOOLS TO LEARN FROM MUSEUMS

HENRY FORD ACADEMY
DEARBORN, UNITED STATES
A MUSEUM SHARES NOT ONLY ITS RESOURCES BUT ITS
HOME WITH A SCHOOL

Active learning occurs when people stretch their minds to interact with the information and experiences at hand. In art museums, visitors are learning actively when they do such things as formulate their own questions about works of art, reflect on their own ideas and impressions, make their own discerning judgments, construct their own interpretations, and seek their own personal connections. These sorts of behaviors are called active learning because they involve acting on available information—including information from one's own thoughts, feelings, and impressions—in order to form new ideas. Research shows that people learn more deeply and retain knowledge longer when they have opportunities to engage actively with the information and experiences at hand, even if these opportunities are punctuated with moments of passive receptivity. This is a general fact about cognition, as true in museums as it is in schools.

As theaters of active learning, museums are distinct from schools in that they make their educational offerings without demand. In museums, visitors are free to move about at their own pace and to set their own agendas. They are free to choose whether to read wall text or take audio tours, free to follow a recommended trail through an exhibition or choose their own path. Museums invite learning rather than require it, which is why they are often called "free choice" or informal learning environments. This discretionary quality of experience is a feature of good learning generally. Research demonstrates that when people have some degree of personal agency—some range of choice about the shape and direction of their own learning activities—learning tends to be more meaningful and robust. In art museums, active learning and personal agency are natural partners. When we're in charge of our own learning, we often do find opportunities to engage our minds, especially in environments rich with evocative objects and experiences. **Adapted from:** "Learning in Museums" **For more:** www.collegeart.org

You could easily get lost in the 12 acres of exhibits at the Henry Ford Museum, in Dearborn, Michigan. Visitors can see the bus where Rosa Parks made her famous protest, the chair Abraham Lincoln sat in when he was assassinated at Ford's Theatre, and thousands of other American artifacts collected by automobile magnate Henry Ford. At the far edge of the museum, visitors come upon what at first looks like another glass-enclosed exhibit. Closer inspection reveals classrooms where high school students study English, math, science, history, and art—just like their peers all across America. The difference: Several times a week, these students put down their books and spread out into the museum and Greenfield Village, the 90-acre site that hosts 82 historic buildings, many collected and reassembled by Ford. For example, freshmen learning to use graphing calculators interview museum visitors about their favorite exhibits and then graph the statistics they've gathered. For a junior-year biology project, students research agricultural methods on the two working farms in the village and use what they learn to design a farm that could function on Mars. **Adapted from:** "Creating Classrooms: It Takes a Village—and a Museum" **For more:** www.edutopia.org

16.

Emulate museums

An environment rich in evocative objects—whether it's a classroom or a museum—triggers active learning by letting students pick what to engage with.

To me, one of the most brilliant things they're doing with the Henry Ford Academy is simply saying, "Look, we have these places in our society that are already rich with culture and content. Why do we build an empty box and then try to make it rich? Why not use an existing asset in our society that's currently often not very well used?" There's an efficiency to that. Five hundred students go to school with hundreds of thousands of objects of material culture. I think that concept could be so easily adapted to so many different kinds of institutions.

—Bruce Mau, BMD

KEY LEARNING COMMUNITY
INDIANAPOLIS, UNITED STATES
THE FLOW CENTER OFFERS A SPACE WHERE STUDENTS
CAN FORGET THAT SCHOOL IS WORK

The Flow Center is designed for students to learn how to be in a state of "flow." What is meant by the term "flow"? It is the state in which you are so involved in an activity that nothing else seems to matter; in which you are totally unaware of your surroundings but enjoying your task; in which you are highly or intrinsically motivated. Sometimes students understand the simpler explanation: "getting into the rhythm of things."

How do we get students intrinsically or self motivated? By offering them activities (games, puzzles, manipulatives, and other challenges) on the multiple intelligences model and by getting them to understand that they can have fun and learn at the same time. We offer a relaxed atmosphere where students are not pressured by the routines of regu-lar class time. By getting students to realize that the thought process used for problem-solving activities in the flow room is the same thought process used in solving problems in other areas of their studies, we encourage them to become productive thinkers.

Adapted from: "Key Learning Community—Flow Theory"
For more: www.ips.k12.in.us

17.
Form follows function

It seems obvious but is often forgotten: Teaching and learning should shape the building, not vice versa.

One of my favorite quotes is from Dieter Rams—
he was head of design at the German manufacturer
Braun. He is called one of the most influential
industrial designers of the 20th century, or at least
the last part of it—he only retired about 10 years
ago. What he said is: "Form has to come after
function, I can't conceive of it in any other way.
There are certainly psychological functions as well,
it is a matter of balancing the aesthetic content
with regard to use."

—Dr. Axel Haberer, VS Furniture

MINISTRY OF EDUCATION NEW HIGH SCHOOLS
CAYMAN ISLANDS

In 2005, the Cayman Islands government made a pledge to transform their country's education system. Leveraging the advantages of a small population and a thriving economy, the Cayman Islands Ministry of Education has embraced the ambition of providing a framework of opportunities for all learners on the Islands, and promoting 21st-century teaching and learning that will equip students to compete on the international stage. With that ambition in mind, OWP/P has been developing a prototype plan for Cayman Islands high schools that is being constructed at three schools. The plan embraces the concept of project-based learning, a learning approach where students develop interdisciplinary skills for living in a knowledge-based, highly technological society.

I came to this job as the permanent secretary in the Ministry of Education of the Cayman Islands with a passion for development. What are the core elements of national development? It doesn't start with the state of our economic health; it starts with the home, and the quality of experience we provide the family. Education is the extent to which all members of the family understand that concept as a process of lifelong learning.

The success of the transformation of an education system is not in the bricks and mortar. It is in your ability to engage the hearts and minds of all stakeholders in the dialogue of a new way of looking at life and defining education. If you use those very clear words about the aspirations you have for the learners who come out of your system, then that's the basis on which you then move to the question, "How do we effect a learning space that will engender these possibilities to occur?" That's very different from, "We need four classrooms and a science lab."

—Angela Martins, Cayman Islands

Diversity of learning spaces allows students to learn based on individual strengths
- Community theme gardens for each academy
- Discovery studio with outdoor spaces for experimentation
- Collaboration studio
- Reflective studio
- Presentation studio
- Lecturing/learning studio
- Seminar room
- Small group and resource area rich with technology and media
- Cafe

Central to the plan for Cayman Islands high schools is the creation of smaller learning communities, called "academies." Each academy is limited to 250 students to allow for a more intimate relationship between learners and teachers and reduce the issues that come with larger schools, such as overcrowding, security, and long commutes.

Every student will have access to readily available technology and inspiring surroundings that exude a strong sense of Caymanian culture, reinforcing the learners' sense of identity and knowledge of local history. Every academy will have specific spaces celebrating the different modes of learning and the different intelligences, including collaborative spaces for group work, quiet spaces for reflective learning, and "discovery rooms" for multi-disciplinary projects. Trung Le, design principal at OWP/P, describes the inspiration for these agile spaces:

"For the reflective spaces, we were inspired by the story of Albert Einstein. In 1905, the year he published his theory of relativity, Einstein was working at the Swiss Patent Office. He wanted to work there because the job was easy and, more importantly, the office was quiet, which gave him an opportunity to think through his ideas. Even for those of us who aren't Einsteins, the reflective mode can be very productive, and many students work well independently. So we've designed a quiet space with personalized furniture, technology, and lighting. It's acoustically private but visually connected to the collaborative space, so there's always a chance for students to see what their peers are doing.

"The Discovery Studio is a space inspired by the idea that creative people, such as Leonardo Da Vinci, use art and science at the same time to make discoveries. So this is where art and science are taking place in the same area. It's a large space; one side is all science lab casework, with water and gas. On the other side, it's all art casework, with storage for art supplies and projects. The space allows students to flow back and forth between rational, logical thinking and something more intuitive and inspired. It's in that integration of science thinking and art thinking that creativity starts to happen. Architectural studios work the same way: There are no divisions between where we draw and where we do spreadsheets; where we make messes and have group discussions. We're taking practices that we know work in real life and bringing them to the kids, which promotes 'design thinking' at an early stage.

"The Design and Technology building is a media-rich, agile, experimental building that includes space for making things, reinforcing the idea that we all learn by doing, an important concept to remember as we shift from the information age to the conceptual age. By the same token, we're treating teachers as professionals, and designing workspaces and meeting space for them where they, too, can share best practices, and embark on project-based learning and teaching." **Adapted from:** Angela Martins interview with Trung Le, OWP/P

18.

Unite the disciplines

Art and science need each other. Discoveries—great and small—happen when the two come together; so give students places for cross-disciplinary work, and who knows what creative genius will flourish.

Stephen Heppell, one of the United Kingdom's leading learning consultants, talks about "mutuality," about the importance of recognizing the connectedness of humanity, and about how we need each other for real learning and understanding to happen. Scientific research is leading the way on this, with projects that require diverse disciplines. For example, there's The Blue Brain Project—it's a research project that's attempting to simulate the micro-circuitry of the cerebral cortex. To understand the workings of the human brain like that, you need neurologists, psychiatrists, cognitive scientists, computer scientists, designers, artists—all of them collaborating. Mutuality is front and center.

—Trung Le, OWP/P

WHAT WE LEARNED AT:
ROBERT JUNGK SECONDARY SCHOOL
BERLIN, GERMANY
THE STUDENTS TELL US WHAT MAKES THEM FEEL
COMFORTABLE AND INSPIRED

"Our ideal learning environment is a cozy oasis, with palm trees such as those found on a beach, a huge poster with a beautiful scene, a fountain, and soft swivel chairs. The blackboard isn't operable, but it's large so we can write on it and learn from it. At the bottom, there is a decorative mural of all the most significant and important buildings in Berlin."

"All the tables are green, with potted plants. That's because green represents nature, and we feel most comfortable when surrounded by a natural environment."

"We want our school to feel more like home—safe, colorful, with lots of natural light."

"Each desk should have a compartment for personal things."

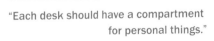

19

Bring the outside in

Transport the community, the landscape, and faraway places into the classroom with visuals and objects that call them to mind.

At Crow Island School in Winnetka, Illinois, Eliel and Eero Saarinen designed each classroom in an L-shape, and placed them side by side, which means there's an alcove of space adjacent to each classroom. Those alcoves are outdoor learning spaces, with tables and chairs—they're like a room with one wall missing and no roof. The effect is that when you're in class, you have the outside pushing in, and when you're outside, you're in class. That's the idea we should shoot for: How can we dissolve the opposition between the man-made and the natural, so that both feel comfortable.

CHAPTER 3

BOD
MOT

Since 2005, schools in Broward County, Florida, have "No Running" signs posted in their playgrounds.

Obesity in children has increased from about 4% in the 1960s to close to 20% in 2004.

By 1998, children under the age of 13 were spending just 25% of their day engaged in unstructured play. In 1981, that figure was 40%.

Children in the fifth and sixth grades can range in height from 4 to 6 feet tall. Just one standard-size seat and desk can't fit this range of students.

I hear and I forget. I see and I remember. I do and I understand.
—Confucius, philosopher

Stringent safety standards have helped to produce play equipment that is lower in height and less challenging than previously designed equipment. This may account for why a study of children using outdoor play spaces at childcare centers found that 87% of the time they were not playing on the equipment.

Sources (top to bottom): Good Magazine, "Fall Down Go Boom"; Centers for Disease Control and Prevention, in Children & Nature Network, Children and Nature 2008: A Report on the Movement to Reconnect Children to the Natural World; University of Michigan Institute for Social Research, in The New York Times, "Children Study Longer and Play Less, a Report Says"; American School & University, "High Class"; Wikiquote, Confucius; Susan Herrington, "Outdoor Spaces," In Schools and Kindergartens: A Design Manual

A study of 500 U.S. teenagers found that 56% of the males and 30% of the females suffered from degeneration of the spine as supported by X-ray evidence.

On average, children of primary school age spend 9 hours per day sitting.

Two European studies found that as many as 60% of schoolchildren experience back problems by the ages of 15 or 16.

If you look at what produces learning and memory and well-being, play is as fundamental as any other aspect of life.
—Stuart L. Brown M.D., president, The National Institute for Play

A rigid sitting posture is manageable for a limited time. However, an exclusively static posture can lead to mental and physical impairment due to poor oxygen supply, causing what can be referred to as "the school headache."

7% of first graders (in the U.S.) now get no recess at all, with many more having their minutes drastically cut; the poorer the school, the less time is dedicated to it.

Sources (top to bottom): Cornell University Ergonomics Web, "Get Techfit" Guidelines; Federal Working Group on the Development of Posture and Exercise, *Ergonomics for children*; Cornell University Ergonomics Web, "Get Techfit" Guidelines; *The New York Times Magazine,* "The Importance of Play"; Federal Working Group on the Development of Posture and Exercise, *Ergonomics for children*; *Good Magazine,* "Fall Down Go Boom"

Watching a child makes it obvious that the development of his mind comes through his movements.

— Maria Montessori

Maria Montessori, the Italian doctor, educator, and founder of the Montessori education method, formulated her theories about child development and her systems for child education by observing disabled children. She continued to watch and work with children of all capacities for the rest of her long life, and wrote over and over again, in books, essays, and speeches, about the role of activity, especially physical activity, in learning. It was a subject on which, she felt, we all had much to learn.

In her last book, *The Absorbent Mind*, first published in 1949 and still in print, she wrote, "When mental development is under discussion, there are many who say, 'How does movement come into it? We are talking about the mind.' And when we think of intellectual activity, we always imagine people sitting still, motionless. But mental development must be connected with movement and be dependent on it. It is vital that educational theory and practice should be informed by that idea."

Although more and more educators do seem convinced that, as Montessori said, "the task of the educator lies in seeing that the child does not confound good with immobility and evil with activity," most of those educators receive little assistance from the physical environments in which they, and the children in their charge, work. Concrete school-yards, cramped classrooms, and fixed furniture all communicate exactly the equation that Montessori warned against. But there is hope, as this chapter testifies. Scientists, researchers, designers, and government policy-makers join educators to offer new evidence that Montessori was right about there being, in her words, an almost mathematical relation-ship between the surroundings, the activity, and the development of the child.

DR. DIETER BREITHECKER
THE BODY-BRAIN CONNECTION

Dr. Dieter Breithecker is a sports and physical scientist and Europe's foremost expert on the relationship between ergonomic design in school furniture and the physical development of school children. Breithecker studied sports and pedagogy at Justus-Liebig-University in Giessen, Germany. Since 1981, he has been with, and is now head of, the Federal Institute on the Development of Posture and Exercise in Wiesbaden. He teaches in the Active School in Germany and Europe. He has published articles, lectures, and videos, most recently on the subject of school dynamics. According to Breithecker, conventional ideas about the physical needs of school children need to be fundamentally rethought.

In your lectures on children and movement, you talk about something you call "the hidden curriculum" of school. Can you describe what that is? First of all, young people, children and adolescents, are really restless. You can observe this every day: Whenever they have a chance, they will romp around, they will climb on things, even when they are sitting they will rock in their chairs. We as adults don't have empathy for all this fidgeting. We say, "Sit up straight. It's good for your posture" and "Sit still and concentrate." It's a deep-rooted kind of teaching, but it's the wrong thing to say.

You've called these instructions that adults give kids "the sitting trap." Yes, because we train kids to learn a behavior that is far from natural. Even as an adult, when you are sitting for a long time you risk sitting-related injury and postural damage. But with kids, it is also a problem for brain development.

You're convinced that if a body is inactive, brain activity is reduced. What persuaded you of that? I know from my own experience as a lecturer that an adult will lose concentration after 25 to 30 minutes.

Well, a child in elementary school will lose concentration after five or, at the most, 10 minutes, and an adolescent after 15 to 20 minutes. We have done a lot of studies with children in schools, in different nations, and we have come to the same result: After the fourth lesson of the morning, no concentration can be maintained. But if someone is getting bored and you ask him to stand up and do an exercise where his vestibular system, his balance system, is challenged—for example, standing on one foot—after five to 10 seconds he will be able to concentrate afterward. When you relate this to a child who starts to rock on a chair, that rocking stimulates the vestibular system too. We have found out that stimulating the balance system activates special hormones, such as neurotrophin, that have a tremendous effect on brain activity. We adults, when we were kids, we used to be active after school, but kids today are moving one hour a day, on average, and sitting eight to 10 hours a day.

You've just mentioned the difference between school children today and a generation ago. Where did you go to school and what was it like?

20.

Make peace with fidgeting

Think of it as brain development, which it is. Then think of how to make room for it in the classroom.

I learned that fidgeting and movement can have a very positive impact on learning by observing my son. He always listened better when his hands were busy. I started reading about this phenomenon in educational journals—this was when Daniel was in fourth grade—and I realized his teacher needed to ease up on him. I had been called to have a parent-teacher conference because, apparently, Daniel was knitting in the back row while his teacher was lecturing up front. To his teacher, this meant Daniel wasn't paying attention. I asked if Daniel was distracting the other kids, or if he was being rude, or doing poorly. I got "no" on all counts. So either the teacher didn't get it, or he didn't like the fact that Daniel was a great knitter! This was back in the 1980s!

—Helen Hirsh Spence, educational consultant to VS Furniture

My sister-in-law is a teacher, and she does a lot of tutoring at home in the summer. She was tutoring her neighbor's son who was always wanting to move, and she said, "You want to move? That's fine." She got out the exercise bike, put it in the living room, and from then on he did all his lessons while he pedaled away on the exercise bike.

—Christine DeBrot, VS Furniture

I went to a traditional school in a lovely rural region of Germany. I was born in 1953, so we didn't have many TV programs and I didn't have a computer. But I had a lot of friends and in the afternoon we were outdoors for five, sometimes, in the summer, six hours a day. And we did, I promise you, a lot of forbidden things because no adults were around! I had the opportunity to walk to school, where kids today are getting to school by school bus or "taxi-mama." But even though I had more movement than the kids of today, I had the same problems at school: After 10 minutes of lesson time, my eyes were vacant, my thoughts were wandering, and

When you go to an office, every employee who has to be productive, who has to be efficient, has a chair he can adjust to his own body proportion.

I couldn't concentrate, so I fidgeted. Today, as a scientist, I know what was happening in my body. My fidgeting stimulated my brain to resist body and mind fatigue. We scientists call this natural rhythmical behavior. It is not gymnastics, it is not a sport activity.

You used to work in sports. Yes, my background is in the movement sciences and I used to focus on sports. I did a research project at the beginning of the '90s with a classroom group. I had everyone sitting on gymnastic balls. The teacher described some students by saying "they really can't sit still, they have typical hyperactivity syndrome." I have found that these kids could learn better while they were sitting in a dynamic way. I realized it is not really necessary, for your health, that you practice a sport activity, but what is necessary is that you move. Today we have parents driving kids to baseball, to football, to soccer, to places where they are educated by a trainer, but we have forgotten basic, essential activities like climbing, balancing, and so on that are necessary for the development of body, mind, and soul.

The problem that you're describing is a very broad socio-cultural one. What can schools do? Let's begin with the basics, with the classroom workstations.

That's interesting you say "workstation." Elsewhere you've described school as a workplace. Why? What do we expect when kids are going to school? We expect them to learn for the future. We expect them to bring home good test scores. We expect them to behave themselves the whole school day. From my point of view that is more concentrated work than some people are doing in the office.

You're right about that! I have seen some school workstations in the States and I know the workstations in Europe, and they are nearly all the same: More than 80 percent of students are not sitting at a workstation that is adjusted to their body size. It's unbelievable! When you go to an office, every employee who has to be productive, who has to be efficient, has a chair he can adjust to his own body proportion.

Why do we seem reluctant to acknowledge that this is also necessary for children? The real problem is money. Money and people who say kids don't have the same problems as adults, they are young and they have rubber bones so they don't get hurt. But we have European research that shows that by the end of elementary school most kids are complaining of headaches. And this is what I cannot understand: When schools are buying new furniture they mostly buy the same old rigid stuff they had before. Please understand this in the right way: That's a kind of child abuse, because we have to be realistic, we won't get kids back climbing trees like I did. When you must buy new furniture because the old furniture is damaged, then please look for furniture that absorbs the movement needs of the sitting body and does not restrict or suppress it. Movement is life, life is movement!

21.

Decide on dynamic

When classroom chairs wear out, invest in new ones that absorb rather than restrict the movements of growing bodies.

CR: We're willing to replace technology frequently — these days if you've had your computer for three years it's considered old and everybody agrees it's time for a new version. But in Germany, school furniture is budgeted to be replaced every 20 years. Therefore the furniture has to last 20 years, no matter whether it's comfortable or not.

CB: One school that was convinced about the benefits of ergonomic furniture took the old furniture, and had the students paint it — the kids made it into art objects. Then the school invited the public in for an auction, and of course the parents would say, "Oh, I want to buy the chair that my child painted," and so the school raised enough money to buy ergonomic furniture.

—Claudius Reckord and Carmen Braun, VS Furniture

PERSPECTIVES CHARTER SCHOOL
CHICAGO, UNITED STATES

AN AMERICAN PILOT PROJECT TESTS CLASSROOM ERGONOMICS

Perspectives Charter School participated in a pilot study with VS Furniture to test the hypothesis that "ergodynamic" desks and chairs would provide better conditions for individual rhythmic movements, and thus a better learning environment, than static furniture.

Three groups of students from grades 6 to 12 were equipped with different furniture. Students in group one sat in traditional static and non-adjustable furniture. Those in group two were furnished with a mix of traditional and ergonomic furniture: non-adjustable chair-desk combinations, free-swinging chairs, and non-inclinable tabletops. Group three's students were given ideal ergonomic standards: continuously height-adjustable chair-desk combina-

tions, inclinable tabletops, and rolling/swivel chairs with rocking mechanisms.

The more adjustable the furniture was, the more frequently students varied their postural behaviors. The results further showed [in "attention endurance" tests designed to record the students' attentiveness and ability to concentrate] that giving students increased opportunity to move while seated—rocking, swiveling, and rolling—triggered far-above-average levels of concentration during test taking. **Adapted from:** Case Study: *Perspectives Charter School, Chicago, Illinois*

22.

Swivel to attention

Give students furniture that lets them twist and lean safely. The movement will increase their ability to concentrate.

I ask people to imagine working for nine hours in a very rigid chair with a desk that's stuck to the chair. I ask them, "Would you like that?" And, of course, you don't get any "yeses" to that, you only get "nos." It turns out that there is scientific evidence for this feeling. Saarland University in Saarbrücken conducted a study investigating how movement effects body temperature. The study found that when you have dynamic seating, you have a higher body temperature. That is a sign of greater blood circulation, which means more oxygen is arriving at the brain, making concentration easier.

—Claudius Reckord, VS Furniture

ENGAGED LEARNING

DESIGNERS ILLUSTRATE HOW FLEXIBLE FURNISHINGS
FREE TEACHERS AND STUDENTS TO BECOME GUIDES
AND LEARNERS

Many schools are moving away from instruction
in which students attend 50-minute lectures,
much of which they will forget as soon as they are
tested on it, if not sooner. The focus has shifted to
learning how to learn. If it is true that people learn
90 percent of their skills on the job, accumulating
facts in school will not benefit them. Instead, they
must know how to retrieve facts quickly.

In an "Engaged Learning Model," the teacher's
role progresses from being the "sage on the stage"
to being the "guide on the side." Instead of a
dispensation of facts, a class session becomes
a participatory gathering of facts. With this model,
classroom organization must now accommodate
periods of direction, guidance, research, sharing,
and summary. The furnishings must be flexible to
support these dynamics and enhance the opportunity for different types of learners to engage a
topic from a perspective that has meaning to them.

Adapted from: "Engaged Learning"

For more: www.asumag.com

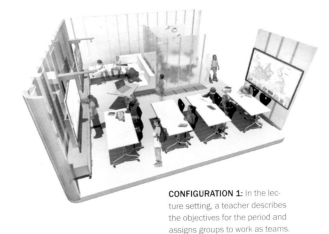

CONFIGURATION 1: In the lecture setting, a teacher describes
the objectives for the period and
assigns groups to work as teams.

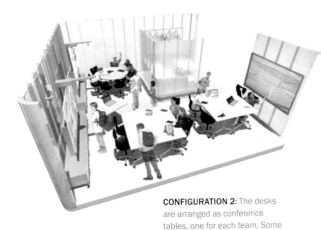

CONFIGURATION 2: The desks
are arranged as conference
tables, one for each team. Some
students may use a computer for
research or graphics; others may
prepare flipchart presentations.

CONFIGURATION 3: Desks are
arranged in a U-shape. Teams
present back to the rest of the
class for feedback and discussion.

23.

Make classrooms agile

A learning space that can be reconfigured on a dime will engage different kinds of learners and teachers.

We hear so much talk about limited resources, not only in terms of money but also in terms of space. OWP/P collaborated with VS on an exercise to answer the question, "What can we do with 400 square feet beyond just setting desks and chairs up in a row?" It is remarkable what you can do if you're given the right kinds of furniture—how agile you can make the space, how media-rich you can make it, how you can engage different modes of learning.

—Trung Le, OWP/P

We use a guideline for all our school furniture: Educators and students have to be able to adjust or reconfigure it themselves, without calling in a facility manager, and they have to be able to do so within three minutes.

—Dr. Axel Haberer, VS Furniture

INVITATION TO PLAY

A U.K. GOVERNMENT GUIDE STATES WHY DESIGNING
WELCOMING PHYSICAL EDUCATION SPACES WILL
ENCOURAGE ALL STUDENTS TO PARTICIPATE

Physical education and school sports play a vital role in allowing young people to test many different and important life skills through playing games. The provision of good facilities allows physical education and sport to be played and enjoyed by the maximum number of pupils.

Because it involves pupils in socially challenging situations where they learn to cooperate with, trust, and rely on one another, good physical education and school sport can improve all markers of personal development, including confidence, body image, and communication skills. Some pupils who lack confidence in other parts of the school curriculum may find a place where they can shine. Where other pupils feel less confident about engaging in physical activity, offering a range of activities in a secure, comfortable, and welcoming environment can help to create a positive attitude to participating in physical education and school sport. Once increased confidence has begun to emerge, the benefits of this can be transferred to other areas of life and of the school curriculum.

New approaches to teaching and learning in physical education and school sport mean that the design of facilities needs to be approached in new ways. They should be exciting and inspiring places to be. They should provide an interesting and high-quality backdrop to pupils' performance, complementing the dynamic movement and activity that takes place within them.

Imaginative use of materials can bring these spaces to life, particularly where there are large floor and wall areas. Color can help to define territories for different sports and games, as well as enliven the often drab surfaces of urban play areas. Using natural daylight reinforces the connection of physical activity and well-being with the natural world.

Creating different degrees of transparency—where light travels through a building—and viewing opportunities will make pupils more aware of the activities that are taking place. Approachable spaces that you can see into will encourage participation, allowing less confident students to see before they try. Areas for observation located near formally marked sports areas allow space for pupils to watch casually, building up confidence to participate more fully at a later time. **Adapted from:** Schools for the Future: Inspirational Design for PE & Sports Spaces **For more:** www.teachernet.gov.uk

24.

Respect fitness facilities

Make them attractive and visible to reinforce the connection between physical activity and overall well-being.

Not every school has to have its own fitness facilities. At a workshop we learned about a school that shared facilities with a YMCA, which had lots of benefits. For instance, the school had the use of a full-size swimming pool, which they wouldn't have been able to afford on their own.

—Carmen Braun, VS Furniture

HAMPDEN GURNEY CHURCH OF ENGLAND PRIMARY SCHOOL
LONDON, UNITED KINGDOM

AN URBAN SCHOOL PROJECT SHOWS HOW TO PROVIDE
PLENTY OF PLAY SPACE ON A SMALL SITE

Hampden Gurney School is a new example of regeneration for urban schools. The creative approach taken to financing the project—selling part of the land for the construction of 52 residential apartments on the site—funded the construction cost of the school building.

Since the residential blocks took up much of the original play area, the challenge for the design team was to maintain the statutory amount of play area in a six-story school. The architects, Building Design Partnership, developed the concept of the multi-level "vertical school" or "children's tower." Students "move up" the school as they progress through the years. The classrooms on each level are linked by

a bridge across a central light well, to open-air play decks that provide safe, weatherproof play and territory for each age group. The result is more play and teaching space on less than a third of the site.

Adapted from: *PEB Compendium of Exemplary Educational Facilities* **For more:** www.oecd.org

25.

Take the "ground" out of "playground"

Who said playgrounds had to be at ground level? Locate play space anywhere and everywhere, from rooftop terraces to indoor atriums.

When I think about my own experience in public school, the playground was a mob scene of kids just running around. They got two 15-minute breaks— one in the morning and one in the afternoon—and the idea was they needed those breaks to burn off energy, because they were required to sit still for the rest of the day in the classroom, concentrating. Of course they couldn't. But if you integrate the idea of play throughout the day and throughout the building, maybe children could function normally.

—*Michael Waldin, BMD*

BRAINS IN MOTION

We must understand how human beings learn and place that understanding at the very center of teaching.

In order to make sense of the vast amount of research that has been generated in fields ranging from clinical psychology and cognitive psychology to biology and neuroscience, educational consultants Renate Caine and Geoffrey Caine developed a set of 12 Brain/Mind Learning Principles that summarize what is presently known about learning. The principles look at all learners as living systems where physical and mental functioning are interconnected.

Principle number one is "All learning engages the physiology." One reason so much traditional teaching involves students sitting in their assigned seats is the belief that the brain is somehow separate from the body and that the body is not very involved in learning. The research on plasticity, as well as brain research in general, tells us that the body and mind are totally interconnected. When a person is appropriately engaged in a complex experience, multiple body/brain/mind systems are integrated, focused and working together naturally. Educators must begin to understand what this principle is saying and how to translate this information into practice. **Adapted from:** *12 Brain/Mind Learning Principles in Action* **For more:** www.cainelearning.com

PLAYGROUNDS AND THE WAR AGAINST OBESITY

There's no ignoring childhood obesity. [In the United States, and increasingly many other western nations] It's a national epidemic that threatens our children's health and, if left unaddressed, will heavily tax health care systems in the future. It's an enemy so persistent and prevalent, roughly one in every six children between the ages of six and 11 are considered dangerously overweight.

It seems that everyone has declared war on childhood obesity. [American] presidential candidates vow to eradicate it if elected. Talk-show hosts try to mobilize stay-at-home moms. Medical experts have made a call to arms.

While these groups all play important roles, they are not on the front lines of the battle. That arduous assignment belongs in part to recreation, sports, and fitness facility managers. They're the ones charged with creating the engaging programs and purchasing the attractive equipment that will get kids moving.

According to Doug Kupper, director of the Parks and Recreation Department for Wichita, Kansas, "The new national studies show that kids are now getting a majority of their exercise on the playground and not through other recreational activities."

Forward-thinking recreation facility managers have made playgrounds ground zero in this winnable war against childhood obesity. Playgrounds offer children opportunities for physical activity on a daily basis, giving them a free place to run, jump, and build muscle. **Adapted from:** *"Pump Up the Fun: What's new on the playground?"*
For more: www.recmanagement.com

26.

Promote healthy play

Consider playgrounds a free place for children to burn calories as well as build motor skills.

Those of us who've run schools in North America have had to deal with a lot of litigation over the past decade, and it's a real shame. Because of it, children's school lives have been so structured that they're under constant supervision. The risk factor has been taken right out of their play, or much of it. Play areas are sanitized so children won't get dirty. Play structures are regulated—material, surfaces, even colors. On the one hand, this is all terrific, but I can't help thinking about some of the advantages of those ugly, rickety old jungle gyms and monkey bars—they did foster creativity and problem-solving. I'm certainly not advocating for unsafe environments, or for children to be endangered in any way. But I do sometimes wonder about the extremes of an overly protective society. How do children benefit, in the long run?

—Helen Hirsh Spence, educational consultant to VS Furniture

CREATING PLAYGROUNDS KIDS LOVE
DESIGNERS AND RESEARCHERS DISCOVER THAT NATURE
IS A CHILD'S MOST IMAGINATIVE PLAYMATE

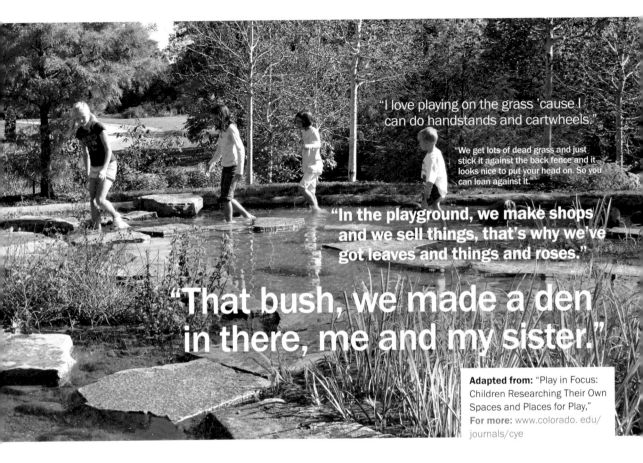

"I love playing on the grass 'cause I can do handstands and cartwheels."

"We get lots of dead grass and just stick it against the back fence and it looks nice to put your head on. So you can lean against it."

"In the playground, we make shops and we sell things, that's why we've got leaves and things and roses."

"That bush, we made a den in there, me and my sister."

Adapted from: "Play in Focus: Children Researching Their Own Spaces and Places for Play," **For more:** www.colorado. edu/ journals/cye

Most of today's adults spent recess on playgrounds that were covered with asphalt and studded with play equipment—such as swings, jungle gyms, and slides—that built their gross motor skills. When it comes to designing playgrounds for today's children, that's what we automatically picture. So we pull out a catalogue, pick out a couple of pieces of playground equipment, and feel pretty good about it. Most of that equipment is much safer and more accessible to all children than it used to be, but it doesn't come close to giving children what they want and need.

When adults are outdoors, they admire a healthy lawn, a nicely tended vegetable garden, and beds of beautiful flowers. When children are outdoors,

they're crawling under bushes, digging in dirt, damming streams, and climbing anywhere their legs and sense of adventure will take them. This is why outdoor areas designed by adults often fail to delight their intended audience. Children want areas filled with nature, from plants, trees, flowers, and water, to animals and insects.
Adapted from: "Creating Playgrounds Kids Love"
For more: www.whitehutchinson.com/children

27.

Naturalize play spaces

Kids don't need much to engage their imaginations. Allowing grass and leafy plants to flourish in play spaces will provide endless opportunities for play and discovery.

When you pave the playground, you take the complexity and richness of living organisms, a huge bandwidth that is fun, and scary, and dynamic, and hugely interesting, and compact it down to nothing. When I visited a school outside Chicago, classes were letting out, and we watched kids as they were going home. Next to the school was a frozen pond. Three or four kids had crawled out onto it and were poking at the ice with a stick. That freedom is one of the sources of an entrepreneurial approach to the world. You learn that you can make things happen. So I think anything that we can do to give children free time and free space in a rich environment that is not determined, not programmed, is a huge asset for them.

—Bruce Mau, BMD

FRIDTJOF NANSEN SCHOOL
HANNOVER, GERMANY

The World Health Organization's Global School Health Initiative is designed to improve the health of children, school personnel, families, and other members of the community, through schools. A "Health-Promoting School" can be characterized as a school constantly strengthening its capacity as a healthy setting for living, learning, and working. There are 10 principles for a Health-Promoting School, including a principle devoted to the school environment: "The health promoting school places emphasis on the school environment, both physical and social, as a crucial factor in promoting and sustaining health." One of the pilot schools in the Health Promoting Schools Network was Fridtjof Nansen School in Hannover, Germany. Several of its key health-promoting projects promote healthy activity in the learning environment.

The school program at Fridtjof Nansen includes five compatible elements:

1. The expression of a new culture of learning, which can be found in the self-learning centers—theme rooms where students can fully experience and understand real phenomena.

2. To play a strong role in the surrounding community, the school uses its position as a center of learning in order to offer and promote a range of activities and cultural events, including judo, rock climbing, wrestling, and team sports. In addition to building stronger bodies, these community offerings help build self-esteem and minimize disruptive behavior.

3. From an organizational standpoint, the school administration has enacted comprehensive quality-assurance standards and innovative time and project management methods.

4. Because a school environment should allow students to both learn effectively and live healthfully, free time and well-designed playgrounds and sports facilities can help promote a child's development in a variety of ways.

5. The demands of a comprehensive health initiative include a more dynamic daily rhythm of classroom activities, a balanced diet, plenty of opportunities for movement and physical expression, and a true ergonomic classroom environment.

Schools that promote activity are realizing that student workspaces must be rethought. A student's workspace must support learning activities, in the same way that a business workspace must support business activities. To measure the benefits of a more ergonomic classroom—including the pedagogical possibilities of new, motion-friendly teaching methods—Fridtjof Nansen School, together with the Ministry of Education of Lower Saxony and the City of Hannover, hosted a four-year study dedicated to exploring the relationship between a student's opportunity for in-class motion and their health, well-being, and classroom performance. VS provided all the ergonomic furniture, including flexible, moveable seating, height-adjustable desks, and work surfaces that could be repositioned.

In order to accurately determine how a more dynamic classroom environment influenced the learning and performance capabilities of the children, the study observed three different classrooms at the school, each incorporating varying degrees of ergonomic furniture, freedom of movement, and dynamic teaching methods. The control group consisted of a neighboring primary school with conventional school furniture. The students were tested on their strength, coordination, and agility, and on their ability to concentrate. Their posture was analyzed from an orthopedic perspective, and their working behavior was monitored by both the teachers and the researchers. At the end of the study, the test group's working behavior was more dynamic, which, combined with the movement-oriented teaching methods that had been used over the four years, had a positive influence on the student's motor processes and posture. In attentiveness endurance tests, the test group also showed considerable increases in concentration.

For children, climbing is a basic need. While climbing, children experience, independently, their own motor abilities and talents, and learn how to overcome fear and gain confidence. In moving between risk and security, high places and low places, open areas and tight spaces, they learn the value of boundary setting and discover strategies for overcoming restrictions. Climbing is important for overall physical development, and contributes to building self-confidence.

Unfortunately, most children in the Fridtjof Nansen School district have little opportunity for climbing, and what opportunity does exist doesn't offer enough challenges to attract children. So, the school has built an interior climbing wall and has installed an exterior "maze of rods." It is a construction of six-meter-long wooden logs that appear to have fallen into position accidentally, like a pile of giant pick-up sticks. Diagonally positioned tree trunks stabilize the logs and offer different combinations of climbing levels. A plastic rope connects the main frame with another trunk, for hand-over-hand grappling. Falls are cushioned by a bed of compressed sand. However, the falling area has not been cleared of tree trunks, to encourage children to evaluate the risks of their situation before deciding to act. The openness of the structure allows children to learn by trial and error, in a self-determined way and at their own speed. **Adapted from:** Adapted from: *The Educational Workplace* and *Physically Active Schoolchildren–alert heads*, and "Mut tut gut! Das wichtige Spiel der kinder mit ihren Grenzen" **For more:** www.bag-haltungundbewegung.de, www.fns-online.de

28.

Scale the wall

Climbing builds kids' motor skills and self-confidence, so don't be afraid to install walls and structures they can clamber up.

I've learned a lot about what to provide and expect with my own kids from the children at Fridtjof Nansen school. I have seen, at the school, that children who have places where they can move, who are allowed the freedom for hands-on experiences, and who know how to take risks, become more self-confident and develop mental and emotional strength. Those early years are decisive!

—Dr. Axel Haberer, VS Furniture

WHAT WE LEARNED AT:
CHICAGO ACADEMY FOR THE ARTS
CHICAGO, UNITED STATES
THE STUDENTS TELL US HOW SCHOOL AND LIFE CONNECT

"Kids spend so much more time at school than they used to. Some of us are here from 8 to 6 every day. A school needs to be more than a school—it really is a home away from home."

"One of the things I really like about my school is that it doesn't feel like a school when I walk into it."

"One of the key things in an education environment, especially for visual arts students, is nature—incorporating views to the outside. It clears your mind and makes you more focused on what you need to do."

"Cafeterias should be fully stocked with foods for all different kinds of people. Healthy foods, vegetarian and vegan foods, a salad bar. And junk food too!"

"We shouldn't be afraid to get the classroom messy. It doesn't necessarily need to be the cleanest (or most organized) place in the world in order for you to learn."

29.
Free choice

Life is full of choices. Prepare kids by giving them a say at school.

The greatest thing you learn when you go to college is how to make decisions. To prepare school kids for that, we have to allow them to make choices. Kids have to be involved in developing their own destiny.

—Rick Dewar, OWP/P

CHAPTER 4

COMM
CONNE

Traditional education can be extremely isolating—the curriculum is often abstract and not relevant to real life, teachers and students don't usually connect with resources and experts outside of the classroom, and many schools operate as if they were separate from their communities. —George Lucas, filmmaker

93% of city officials say that the quality of education is very important to the well-being of cities.

In many communities, access to schools is restricted in order to protect the children.
—Tracey Burns, education analyst

Studies of juvenile delinquency and high school drop-out rates demonstrate that a child is better off in a good neighborhood and a troubled family than he or she is in a troubled neighborhood and a good family. —Malcolm Gladwell, journalist and author

While 9 in 10 Americans think that all youth should have access to after-school programs, two-thirds say it is difficult to find programs locally.

Americans recognize that public schools are the heart of their communities. They are at least five times more likely to cite public schools than churches, hospitals, or libraries as their most important local institutions.

Sources (top to bottom): *Edutopia, The George Lucas Educational Foundation*, "A Word from George Lucas: Edutopia's Role in Education"; National League of Cities, Institute for Youth, Education, and Families, "K-12 School Improvement: Why Municipal Leaders Make Education a City Priority"; *Journal of Educational Change*, "Learning and teaching, schools and communities"; Malcolm Gladwell, *The Tipping Point: How Little Things Can Make a Big Difference*; U.S. Department of Education, *21st Century Community Learning Centers: Providing Quality Afterschool Learning Opportunities for America's Families*; National League of Cities, Institute for Youth, Education, and Families, *Action Kit for Municipal Leaders: Improving Public Schools*

Both the fortress and bubble schools are based on the premise that communities, particularly those in challenging urban contexts, have low social capital. —Kathryn Riley, professor and author

While 71% of adult Americans say they walked or rode a bike to school when they were a child, today less than two in ten (17%) school-age children walk.

It takes a village to educate a child.
—African proverb

Urban educators get so beat up and accused of negligence when students don't succeed, but the whole community, the whole village, has to be responsible for the education of our children.
—Dr. Reginald Mayo, superintendent

The percentage of children who live within a mile of school and who walk or bike to school has declined by nearly 25% in the last 30 years. Barely 21% of children today live within one mile of their school.

[My family] believed in the public school because they believed in a community. —Garrison Keillor, broadcaster

Sources (top to bottom): Journal of Educational Change, "Can schools successfully meet their educational aims without the clear support of their local communities?"; Belden Russonello & Stewart Research and Communications, *Americans' Attitudes Toward Walking and Creating Better Walking Communities; Wikipedia, The Free Encyclopedia,* "It Takes a Village"; National League of Cities, Institute for Youth, Education, and Families, *Stronger Schools, Stronger Cities;* Centers for Disease Control and Prevention, in Children & Nature Network, *Children and Nature 2008;* National Education Association, "American Education Week, November 11–17, 2007 Education Quotes"

I believe that the school is primarily a social institution …I believe that education, there-fore, is a process of living and not a preparation for future living.

— John Dewey

No book on education would be complete without John Dewey. A visionary American philosopher, educator, and social critic, Dewey wrote about many aspects of life but is perhaps best known now for his beliefs, books, and projects on education. Education, Dewey wrote, is the fundamental method of social progress and reform.

To a 21st-century reader, the essay in which Dewey wrote those lines, "My Pedagogic Creed," can be both exciting and startling. Exciting because it is such a clear and compelling call to educational reform, and startling because this progressive platform was laid out more than 100 years ago. Dewey argues that much of education fails because it neglects the principle that school is a real and vital form of community life, and instead conceives of it as a place where lessons are to be learned and habits formed. As a result, says Dewey, schools fail to become part of the life experience of the child and so do not truly educate.

That will likely sound all too familiar. Many of our schools are still conceived of in the limited way Dewey laments, and are separated from their communities by long highways, limited hours, inflexible spaces, and, most of all, blinkered vision about the myriad ways in which schools can and should be part of the social ecosystem, in the process enriching both students and communities. A small but inspiring collection of strategies for school-community symbiosis are detailed in this chapter. Parents, educators, and designers from around the world offer anecdotes, evidence, and ideas. Their testimony proves the relevance and necessity of planning, designing, and building schools that are as vital and interconnected as life itself.

LINDA SARATE
IT TAKES A VILLAGE TO BUILD A SCHOOL

Linda Sarate has lived in Little Village, on Chicago's West Side, for most of her life and has been involved in her community as a local school council member at Gary Elementary School and as a community board member at both the Dr. Jorge Prieto Community Health Center and the Little Village Community Development Corporation. Although stricken with polio as a child, Linda has fought for her community whenever she was needed, and has raised three children. She participated in the hunger strike of 2001 that won Little Village and North Lawndale their new high school campus. This is her story of that battle for her children and her community.

If you were taking a visitor on a tour of Chicago's Little Village, what would you want to show them so they could begin to understand your community? Oh, everything! Especially 26th Street—that's our main strip. It's got everything you can buy. There's great food. Mexican health food stores—in the [Mexican American] culture there are a lot of herbs and teas that people drink to help them with different things. There are boutiques, grocery stores. People come from all over and walk up and down 26th Street for everything they need.

In addition to that great shopping strip, Little Village has had a high school for a long time, hasn't it? Yes. It's about 100 years old. It was the only high school in the area. They have great programs there, but the school has its issues. It's in the middle of a gang area. And a lot of kids, either walking to, walking from, or within the building itself, have been beaten up. My nephew went for orientation. The night after orientation, somebody called him up and told him, "If you go back to school tomorrow, you're going to get killed." So my sister put him in another school, of course [in another neighborhood]. There's an invisible bound-ary line and if you cross it you have your life in your hands. That's one of the reasons Little Village needed another high school: so there'd be less tension, less chance of the kids getting hurt.

CPS (Chicago Public Schools) had already bought a parcel of land in Little Village, and they had cleared it, some time before you got involved. When you first talked to CPS, what were you told about why nothing had been built there? We were told, "There's no money." But we knew, by their own admission, that there had been $25 million set aside. They committed themselves by buying the land and clearing it off. They told us, "Well, we used that money for another project." We had a series of public meetings, and we asked CPS to come out. They came with two separate models of what the school could look like. They said, "If you're in this much of a rush to get your high school, and you can't wait until we get more money, then here: take your pick." But each model held only 800 students. The school my son went to alone graduated almost 200 students every year, and there are 8 or 10 "feeder" schools in the neighborhood. The high school would have opened up overcrowded. So we

30.

Build close to home

All children have a right to a school in their own neighborhood.

BM: I've noticed something about the neighborhood in Chicago where my kids go to school: The school system seems to be planned so that, no matter what age you are, your school is located within walking distance appropriate to your age. There are lots of little schools for the little kids, so if you're in grade one, your school is walking distance for you as a six-year-old. And because there are progressively fewer middle schools and high schools, it's as though as the child grows, the distance she has to travel to school grows. Which makes sense.

CR: In Germany, you take a good education for granted. You have the public school system and you expect it to function very well; you simply send your kids to the school in your neighborhood. When I moved to the United States from Germany, I was surprised to find you have a public school system, you have a Catholic school system, you have another religious school system, you have private schools. And as a parent, you wonder, "Okay, what do we do now with our kids?" Where you want to send your kid determines where you buy a house. I had never had to think about that before.

—Bruce Mau, BMD and Claudius Reckord, VS Furniture

told them, "No, that's unacceptable." We started talking about an action. We wanted to do something peaceful that was going to be eye-opening, and we came up with a hunger strike.

The hunger strike lasted for 19 days, until it started to become a danger to the health of the strikers. By the time it had ended, what effect had the strike had? Days after it ended, we got a call from CPS, from the new CEO. The old one had resigned during the hunger strike. We didn't get a 100 percent commitment, but we got 75–80 percent. Which was very well received. But we told

We had camped out right across the street from the school site. It was like a 24-hour celebration. People came out; they sang songs; they told stories.

him we were not going to take this slight victory and walk away from it; we were going to stick by it. And we did. Because we didn't just get a commitment from CPS, we had also woken up the neighborhood. We had camped out right across the street from the school site. It was like a 24-hour celebration. People came out; they sang songs; they told stories; the older people in the neighborhood remembered when they used to fight for things too. Parents would tell us, "Oh, thank you." And we'd say, "Don't thank us yet. We have a lot to do and a long way to go."

Why did your group insist on being part of the entire planning process? Because we didn't want them to just come in and tell us what we needed. We need our kids to know the basics—reading, writing, math—but we also want them to learn about their culture. Culture is very important. And if we were not involved, I don't think that the school would reflect the neighborhood as well. We asked for a lot!

What are some of the things that you asked for? A dance studio for folkloric dancing. We wanted an Olympic-sized swimming pool, because we need our school to be open after hours. We have very limited park space in our neighborhood. This was somewhere to go, something to do, somewhere to

be safe. And we've already had a couple of training programs for parents at the school—computer training and English classes—that was part of our mission too.

How do you think the school and the work that you did to get it built has changed the community? The kids, they love the school. That I know. My son was one of the first students. Well, he was part of it from the beginning. He would go with me on demonstrations, picketing. I think he feels really great that he was there and part of it, because since the first day of school, he has not missed a day. I'm so proud every time I say that! A teenager not wanting to miss school!

The alderman for Little Village had been fighting to get the school built for a couple of years before you got involved. Why do you think that a group of parents were able to get more than elected officials? Because that's what we were—just regular, ordinary, neighborhood people, who took the lead, who decided to say, "Okay, we're not going to stand for this any longer. Our children mean a lot to us, and they have to mean something to you." We don't need a school made of gold—that's not what we were looking for. We were just looking for a good education for our kids, so they can have opportunities that we never had. They should be allowed that chance.

31.

Let your grassroots show

To rally support for a new school, establish a visible presence for the campaign in your community.

I'd like to recommend a movie: *Freedom Writers* is a true story about a teacher in Long Beach, California, a very racially divided community. The teacher, Erin Gruwell, started a project in her classroom that ended up improving an entire neighborhood. The movie is based on the book that Erin put together with her students. It's called *The Freedom Writer's Diary: How a Teacher and 150 Teens Used Writing to Change Themselves and the World around Them*.

—Carmen Braun, VS Furniture

A SHORT HISTORY OF AMERICAN PUBLIC EDUCATION

A HISTORICAL OVERVIEW REVEALS SCHOOL'S STARRING
ROLE IN THE GROWTH OF A NATION

When the U.S. nation's founders set aside the 16th section of townships to produce funds to build schools, there was no curriculum, no image, and no clearly defined student body for these schools. Our core educational values date back to the days of the early republic, a predominantly agricultural environment, but much of the large-scale impetus for the development of a national public school system came through urban, industrial growth and then postindustrial decentralization.

In the early 20th century, architects such as Dwight H. Perkins began the movement to design public schools as urban neighborhood centers tied to the dense urban fabric. The idea of the school as a tool of social reform is not new. The workings of such schools—the mass production of a minimally educated population and the building of petit-monuments to the acquisition of specifically American knowledge—are a legacy of early 20th-century urban ideals. At the same time, however, educational leaders such as John Dewey began to focus on the child as a learning being, rather than an empty vessel for the reception of American values or the trained tool of industrial productivity. The continuing reconfiguration of the landscape, from dense cities into large urban regions, compels us to rebuild and more fully utilize these vital institutions of democratic life.

The accessibility of large quantities of undeveloped land allowed suburban schools to take on more "campus-like" forms. Streetcar and railroad suburbs could not have been conceived without the development of schools to absorb the youth of this family-centered culture. After World War II, schools were an important component in the planning of the Levittown communities [America's first mass-produced suburbs]. Developer William Levitt stated the case succinctly: "A school has to be ready when the house is ready. It's as important as a water main." The sociologist Herbert Gans discovered that the politics of education created the greatest conflict among the Levittowners. Indeed, in postwar America, schools, and particularly the distance to them, were a critical component of the neighborhood unit. To the extent that urban diversity existed, schools were this diversity's common denominator.

Adapted from: *Schools for Cities: Urban Strategies*

For more: www.nea.gov

32.

Build for change

School buildings can be tools for social change, and history's the proof. Take courage and inspiration from what's been done before.

Program 2000 is a wholistic planning initiative in Vienna. In the peripheral areas of the city, the way they are dealing with the issues of sprawl and an influx of new immigrants is to build schools first and allow neighborhoods to grow up around them— schools are becoming the kind of community anchors that churches used to be.

—Trung Le, OWP/P

NEW COLUMBIA COMMUNITY CAMPUS
NORTH PORTLAND, UNITED STATES
THE JURY IS IN ON A SCHOOL THAT COLOCATED WITH TWO
OTHER COMMUNITY SERVICES

It didn't have a name. No one was sure what it would look like. They simply called it the "new elementary school." But, despite its lackluster label, architects and school officials knew this school would be anything but typical. It was 2004, and construction was under way at New Columbia, an 82-acre housing development in North Portland, Oregon. Built on the former site of Columbia Villa, a housing project constructed in 1942 for World War II defense workers, it would have twice the number of units than that of its predecessor. Of concern to Portland Public Schools (PPS) officials was how to accommodate an influx of new students into two existing neighborhood schools—Ball Elementary and Clarendon Elementary—neither of which had the necessary capacity. At Ball, a deteriorating building structure compounded the issue. A new school was needed, but the district had little capital for construction.

PPS and the Housing Authority of Portland were joined by architects and Portland Parks and Recreation to investigate several options. Out of their collaboration emerged the "community campus" concept. The campus would consist of a new Boys and Girls Club, a remodeled/renovated community center, and a new school, which would eventu-

ally be known as Rosa Parks School. Each facility would include shared spaces and offer services to students, their parents, and the community, and, by doing so, reduce the total project cost. **Adapted from:** "Textbook Tech" **For more:** www.architechmag.com

In 2007, the American Architectural Foundation (AAF) and KnowledgeWorks Foundation chose Rosa Parks School at New Columbia Community Campus as the winner of that year's Richard Riley Award for Schools as Centers of Community. "This school is a national model for how the creative design of a school can help to revitalize an entire neighborhood," said Ronald E. Bogle, president and CEO of the American Architectural Foundation. "It is a fantastic example for other school districts, showing how multiple partners can work together and provide a strong intergenerational focus." The jury also singled out Rosa Parks School at New Columbia Community Campus because the design supports small learning environments, makes a variety of services available to the entire community, and has received a Gold LEED certification for sustainability. **Adapted from:** "American Architectural Foundation and Knowledgeworks Foundation Announce winner of 2007 Richard Riley Award" **For more:** www.archfoundation.org

33.
Move in together

Building a new school is an opportunity to make friends with other community services, such as libraries and recreational facilities, and perhaps even make a new home together on a single campus.

At the same time as funding for new schools is becoming more limited, the population is getting older. Just 20 percent of Americans now have kids in school. You have to find a reason for older people to support schools. Building in community amenities is a way to solidify a school campus as a community center that a wide range of people will support. Why do you need to go to a library over there, and then go to an athletic club over there, when you can do it all in that one place? Once you get past the challenge of realizing that you're going to allow adults to share space with kids, there are endless opportunities.

—Rick Dewar, OWP/P

EVANGELISCHE COMPREHENSIVE SCHOOL
GELSENKIRCHEN-BISMARCK, GERMANY
A GERMAN ARCHITECT IMAGINES CHILDREN DESIGNING A SCHOOL, THEN TURNS THAT VISION INTO REALITY

Schnitt F4

In the late 19th century, in the Ruhr area of Germany, an industrial suburb called Gelsenkirchen-Bismarck developed around a coalmine. In the 1990s, Fritz Sundermeier, a visionary educationalist, conceived the idea of catalyzing the redevelopment of the suburb by building a multicultural school and cultural center promoting ecological education. An architectural competition was launched.

Architect Peter Hubner won the competition with a written story that imagined the outcome, decades later, of his proposal. The story took the form of a hypothetical speech given in the year 2034 by a character named Kemal Özcül, who recounts how, as a child, he took part in the building of classrooms, housing, communal facilities, and ecological garden in a collaborative process involving teachers, pupils, the local community and outside professionals.

"At the beginning of the school year, architects, engineers, landscape architects and ecologists arrived at the school to present the whole remarkable project. We were told that we 134 boys and girls were going to build our own school, our own garden, our own world. We were full of the naïve optimism of childhood, our teachers were young and open-minded, and planners coaxed us on with their overwhelming enthusiasm, so that we thought of nothing but our new school ... Nearly all the pupils were so taken with the excitement of building that they stayed long after school, remaining until late in the evening if the weather was good. My uncle Mehmet set up a kebab stall to cater for those whose parents had not sent them out with a picnic. From the balcony of the staff floor, Mrs. Kräutermayer could look down on the roof of our canteen where she had planted a herb garden. This not only served our kitchens, but a market stall, which we ran on Saturdays ... Life together was self-regulating, as in a town that has grown up by itself, letting the houses come together harmoniously with the minimum of rules."

After winning the competition with this story, Peter Hubner did enlist the help of area children to design the school. **Adapted from:** *Evangelische Gesamtschule Gelsenkirchen-Bismarck: Kinder Bauen Iher Schule / Children Make Their Own School*
For more: www.plus-bauplanung.de

34.

Imagine like a child

Visualize a proposed school from a student's perspective — the poignancy of that point of view may help transform a proposal into a built project.

There's an elementary school in Cranbrook, Illinois, called the Vlasic Early Childhood Center, designed by Peter Rose. It is the sweetest little piece of architecture on a child's scale. It's not on an American scale at all — it's like a house in a medieval town in Italy or England that works for adults and for children because it's at that odd in-between scale. But everything in the Center has actually been thought through from a children's standpoint: how you move through the space, what you see, the vista points, the materials. It's the most beautiful example I've seen in contemporary architecture of this idea.

—Elva Rubio, BMD

SCHOOLYARDS AS TOOLS FOR NEIGHBORHOOD REVITALIZATION

A COALITION OF COMMUNITY INTERESTS BUILDS NEW PLAYGROUNDS TO REBUILD CIVIC PRIDE

In 1994, a group called the Urban Land Use Task Force, funded by Boston area foundations, held a series of meetings to discuss Boston's open spaces. The need for "clean, safe and green" schoolyards moved to the very top of the Task Force's agenda. The Task Force approached Boston Mayor Thomas M. Menino, and with the mayor's enthusiastic support, the result was the creation of the Boston Schoolyard Initiative in 1995. Within six years, half of the city's public schools and every neighborhood in Boston were participating in the initiative.

While the most obvious product of any schoolyard project is the newly constructed schoolyard itself, a less tangible but equally important product is the process that moves the project forward. Every potential user and stakeholder is invited into the process at the earliest possible stage. This includes, most especially, each school's students, but also parents, educators, administrators, custodians, before- and after school programs, summer camps, local merchants and business partners, crime watch groups, senior citizen groups, community-based organizations, and neighborhood residents. Together, these stakeholders attend a series of community meetings to assess local needs, develop a consensus about the design of capital improvements, raise funds, and consider how to create a system that will support sustainable schoolyard development.

When the Boston Schoolyard Initiative began its work, a survey of Boston's 128 public schoolyards revealed an appallingly neglected patchwork of broken pavements, torn fences, compacted soil, and hazardous play equipment. Degraded school grounds had contributed to a sense of malaise and urban blight throughout the city. Most alarmingly, their poor condition was sending messages to students and to all local youth that they were simply not a priority. Today, negative conditions and messages have been replaced by a new era of hope. Renovated, attractive and useful schoolyards are acting as positive "tipping points" for the revitalization of entire communities, and negative attitudes have been replaced by feelings of excitement and optimism. **Adapted from:** "Designing Schoolyards & Building Community" **For more:** www.schoolyards.org

35.

Consult widely and early

Those heading up the planning process for a new school will get off on the right foot by inviting every potential user and stakeholder into the process — right from the start.

There are very simple things you can do during the design process to heal separations that occur naturally. When we were working on a new school in Carbondale, Illinois, we had really good community engagement, great conversations going on with people from the library, the mayor's office, two school districts, the park district. They were all at the table together—for the first time. They were saying to one another, "You know, you have this, and I could really use that." Design got them talking together about their needs and what they could share.

—Rick Dewar, OWP/P

BUILDING A SCHOOL, RECONSTRUCTING A COMMUNITY

A SCHOOL AND AN APPROACH TO LEARNING RISE UP FROM THE RUBBLE OF WAR

Reggio Emilia is the name of a town in northern Italy. It is known internationally for its schools, founded on the philosophy that all children are different. Here, in the words of one of its pioneers, pedagogue Loris Malaguzzi, is the origin of the schools.

The history of our approach, and of my place in it, started six days after the end of the Second World War. It was the spring of 1945. I heard that in a small village called Villa Cella, a few miles from the town of Reggio Emilia, people decided to build and run a school for young children. That idea seemed incredible to me! I rushed there on my bike and I discovered that it was all quite true. I found women intent upon salvaging and washing pieces of brick. The people had gotten together and had decided that the money to begin the construction would come from the sale of an abandoned war tank, a few trucks, and some horses left behind by the retreating Germans. "The rest will come," they said to me. "I am a teacher," I said. "Good," they said. "If that is true, come work with us."

It all seemed unbelievable: the idea, the school, the inventory consisting of a tank, a few trucks, and horses. They explained everything to me: "We will build the school on our own, working at night and on Sundays. The land has been donated by a farmer; the bricks and beams will be salvaged from bombed houses; the sand will come from the river; the work will be volunteered by all of us." "And the money to run the school?" A moment of embarrassment and then they said, "We will find it." Women, men, young people—all farmers and workers, all special people who had survived a hundred war horrors—they were all dead serious.

Within eight months, the school and our friendship had set down roots. What happened at Villa Cella was but the first spark. Other schools were opened on the outskirts and in the poorest sections of town, all created and run by parents. Finding support for the school, in a devastated town, rich only in mourning and poverty, would be a long and difficult ordeal, and would require sacrifices and solidarity now unthinkable. When seven more schools were added in the poor areas surrounding the city to the "school of the tank" at Villa Cella, we understood that the phenomenon was irreversible.

When we started to work with these courageous parents, we felt both enthusiasm and fear. We knew perfectly well how weak and unprepared we were. We took stock of our resources—not a difficult task. More difficult was the task of increasing those resources. And even more difficult was to predict how we would use them with the children. We were able to imagine the great challenge, but we did not yet know our own capabilities nor those of the children. We informed the mothers that we, just as the children, had much to learn. A simple, liberating thought came to our aid, namely that things about children and for children are only learned from children. We knew how this was true and at the same time not true. But we needed that assertion and guiding principle; it gave us strength and turned out to be an essential part of our collective wisdom. It was a preparation for 1963, the year in which the first Reggio Emilia municipal schools came to life. **Adapted from:** *The Hundred Languages of Children*
For more: www.reggioalliance.org

36.

Roll up your sleeves

A new school will be realized faster if parents pitch in to make it happen.

TL: The Rogers Park Montessori school in Chicago had been renting space at a church. An architect at our firm was sending his daughter there and offered to help build a new school. He helped them with everything from site selection to construction supervision. The thing is, all the funds for the new school were raised by the parents.

RD: Most private schools generally begin with a group of concerned parents who want to start a school for a specific reason—for example, religion or language.

AH: At Waldorf schools, there's always a lot of parental involvement; you can even see parents painting a classroom on a Saturday.

—*Trung Le and Rick Dewar, OWP/P and Dr. Axel Haberer, VS Furniture*

ROSA PARKS ELEMENTARY SCHOOL
REDMOND, UNITED STATES

A COMMUNITY DESIGNS NOT ONLY A SCHOOL BUT ALSO THE
PATHS CHILDREN WALK TO GET THERE

This school in King County, just north of Seattle, opened in 2006, dedicated to the 50th anniversary of Rosa Parks' refusal to give up her seat at the front of a public bus to a white man. Martin Luther King spearheaded a bus boycott, which led to desegregation in the United States, and Parks became a national symbol of civil rights.

However, students at the new Rosa Parks Elementary School may never board the kind of bus once ridden by its famous namesake. In fact, the school doesn't even have a traditional school bus stop. Although there is an area for a bus to stop for field trips, and a large "park and ride" about one-quarter mile away, the school is not normally serviced by buses, and students are encouraged to walk or bicycle to school.

Designed to meet the interests of an environmentally committed neighborhood on Redmond Ridge, the school is connected to nearby homes by a series of walking and bicycle trails. Every day volunteers meet students at set times at designated points along the trails for a "walking bus" trip to the school. Students can join at the starting points or anywhere along the route.

The planning process for the school began with a public workshop attended by people living in the 900-home community, which had already established neighborhood design standards that called for pocket parks, large swaths of green belts, and undisturbed forests connected by walking trails. The standards seek a "national park ambiance" that features natural materials, colors, and plantings. The school's design recalls the simplicity of national park architecture in its clean shapes, sloped shed roofs, large view-oriented windows, Douglas fir ceilings, and natural colors of deep brown and charcoal gray. The library, commons, and gymnasium are all accessible after hours and, as the largest public building in the neighborhood, the structure has become an important community asset. **Adapted from:** "Rosa Parks Elementary School Students Walk, Bicycle Rather Than Take the Bus"

For more: www.edcmag.com

37.
Blaze the way

School can start at a student's front door, if the commute is designed as well as the building. Walking paths and bicycle trails connect a school with the homes it serves.

In my hometown, I walked to school, and kids there today still walk or bike to school. That's something almost impossible in the United States, because of fear. Of course parents in Germany are also concerned about their children, but, for example, in my hometown there is a big road school children have to cross. So there are parents at that street, and they guide the kids safely across.

—Claudius Reckord, VS Furniture

I walked to school here in the United States. The rule in our district was that if it was less than a mile, or if you didn't have to cross a busy street, you walked, because the routes were protected by the parents along the way. There were enough kids in the neighborhood that parents would look out the window and watch the kids walking by. Now it's easier for parents to drive to school, so the kids that walk aren't protected or cared for by the neighborhood.

—Rick Dewar, OWP/P

MICHELLE SAKAYAN
CREATING A COMMUNITY FOR
SOUTH AFRICAN SCHOOLGIRLS

Michelle Sakayan is the founder of Sakayan Inc., a consulting firm facilitating programming, planning, design, and management for schools and charitable foundations. She has a Master's of Architecture and began her career working at Nagle Hartray Architects in Chicago, where she specialized in K-12 education projects. While at Nagle Hartray, she worked with South African architects Jeremy Rose and Jonty Doke of Mashabane Rose Architects to realize the 26-building campus and mission of the Oprah Winfrey Leadership Academy for Girls, designed to nurture, educate, and turn gifted South African girls from impoverished backgrounds into the country's future leaders.

I think of an architect as a civil servant, and school design as a social act. You're working with a community, and reflecting their needs. I'm really interested in making sure that the mission and the culture of a school shines through in the architecture, that it becomes a mirror of what the teachers, the students, the parents, and the administrators are trying to do there in their daily lives.

The architectural design of the Leadership Academy for Girls was our response to Oprah Winfrey's dream and mission. This is a college preparatory school, a place to challenge local girls to go to college, and to take their knowledge either back to the town where they're from or to other parts of the world. The school aims to foster the girls' respect and appreciation for their own cultures and for the cultures of others. We went into the communities the girls would be coming from, visited schools, talked to kids. We made sure that the architecture responded not only to the dream and the mission but also to who the girls are.

Girls in South Africa, at this age, sit in circles. Boys sit in lines. Girls love circles, for singing and dancing too. They start chanting, and it becomes really rhythmic and contagious. So, on the campus, the buildings wrap around, like arms hugging, to make outdoor living rooms, spaces that encourage the girls to feel comfortable in circular gatherings. Every classroom opens onto a garden. It fans out, and beyond it are trees. We've mounded the earth under them into small hills that will seat at least 20 people, so that classes can be held outside. This takes advantage of the climate, and embraces the beauty of the South African landscape.

We want the school to be emblematic of South Africa because we want the girls to be proud of their heritage. We used scratched plaster, which is very common in the countryside here: Incredible patterns are scraped into the mud floors and walls of the roundevals, the traditional houses, so we did scratching here too, in a modern way. The girls are coming from 10 different cultural groups. Each culture has beadwork associated with it—anyone who is from South Africa can look at beadwork and say, "that's Zulu," or "that's Tsoto." In the middle of the campus, right in front of the dining hall, which is a popular place to sit, we put 10 columns. Each of the columns is decorated with one of the 10 culture's beadwork, translated into mosaic. It's become a landmark, a place of respect showing each girl that she's important, no matter where she's coming from.

38.
Make them proud

The rich cultural traditions of a school's students offer design opportunities. Embracing them is a mark of respect that tells students that where they come from matters as much as where they're going to.

The last school where I was headmistress was an all girls' independent school in Ottawa, Canada's capital. The school had a very international flavor, partly because Canada is a very multicultural society, and also because of the diplomatic presence in Ottawa—there are embassies all over the city. To acknowledge where the girls came from, we'd hang their national flags in the main foyer. The tradition started when the school was small. All the flags were put in alphabetical order, high up in the atrium. Every time a girl left the school, or a new girl arrived, a flag had to be taken down or added. Our custodial staff was very accommodating, but this did cause them endless grief. Nevertheless, we all felt that it was well worth it! The flags were a signal to anyone who studied in the school, or worked there, or even visited, that we were a diverse student body and proud of it!

—Helen Hirsh Spence, educational consultant to VS Furniture

CHICAGO PUBLIC SCHOOLS
CHICAGO, UNITED STATES

Chicago Mayor Richard Daley: Chicago is known for its beautiful lakefront, its dramatic skyline, and its outstanding architecture. But Chicago is much more than that. It's a city of neighborhoods. Much of my work as mayor consists of using the tools of government to create the conditions that can lead to healthy, livable, thriving communities. So how does government help build stronger neighborhoods? You don't tear down the old one and build something new on top. That's been tried and it generally hasn't worked. You start by building what I call community anchors: schools, libraries, parks, and police and fire stations. The most important anchor, by far, is the school.

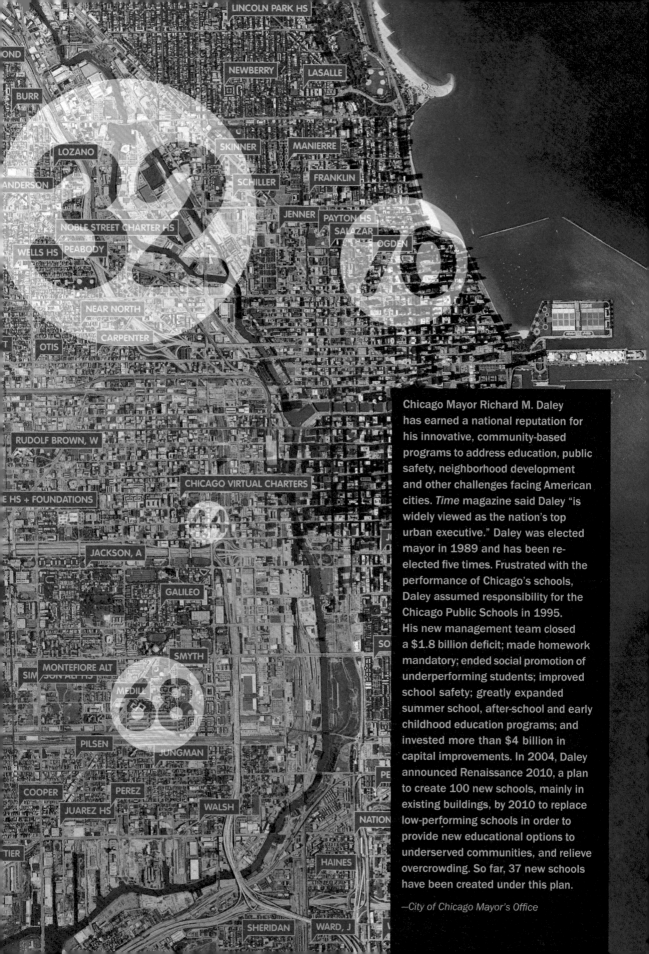

LINCOLN PARK HS

OND

BURR

LOZANO

ANDERSON

NEWBERRY   LASALLE

SKINNER   MANIERRE

SCHILLER   FRANKLIN

NOBLE STREET CHARTER HS

WELLS HS   PEABODY

NEAR NORTH

CARPENTER

OTIS

JENNER   PAYTON HS
          SALAZAR
          OGDEN

32, 70

RUDOLF BROWN, W

E HS + FOUNDATIONS

CHICAGO VIRTUAL CHARTERS

JACKSON, A

GALILEO

MONTEFIORE ALT

SIM   SON ALT HS

MEDILL

SMYTH

68

PILSEN

JUNGMAN

COOPER   PEREZ

JUAREZ HS   WALSH

NATION

TIER

HAINES

SHERIDAN   WARD, J

Chicago Mayor Richard M. Daley
has earned a national reputation for
his innovative, community-based
programs to address education, public
safety, neighborhood development
and other challenges facing American
cities. *Time* magazine said Daley "is
widely viewed as the nation's top
urban executive." Daley was elected
mayor in 1989 and has been re-
elected five times. Frustrated with the
performance of Chicago's schools,
Daley assumed responsibility for the
Chicago Public Schools in 1995.
His new management team closed
a $1.8 billion deficit; made homework
mandatory; ended social promotion of
underperforming students; improved
school safety; greatly expanded
summer school, after-school and early
childhood education programs; and
invested more than $4 billion in
capital improvements. In 2004, Daley
announced Renaissance 2010, a plan
to create 100 new schools, mainly in
existing buildings, by 2010 to replace
low-performing schools in order to
provide new educational options to
underserved communities, and relieve
overcrowding. So far, 37 new schools
have been created under this plan.

—*City of Chicago Mayor's Office*

When I became mayor, I inherited a public school system that had been run by a separate branch of government, over which the mayor had relatively little control. The school system was underperforming and school buildings were literally falling apart, with broken windows, leaky roofs, peeling paint, inadequate heating systems, and crowded classrooms.

Those schools sent some very clear messages to the community. They told the children that we didn't take education seriously. They told neighborhood residents, "The schools don't maintain their property. Why should you maintain yours?"

So I got the law changed in 1995 to give the mayor personal responsibility for the Chicago Public Schools. We persuaded Chicagoans to raise their taxes to finance more than $4 billion of school construction and repair. In addition to building 118 new schools, additions, and annexes, we have torn out 100 asphalt playgrounds and turned them into campus parks for students and neighborhood residents. This has brought the residents closer to the schools, both literally and figuratively.

The object is to make our city a place where people live because they want to, not because they have to. If people want to live in your city, all sorts of good things happen. They take better care of their property, and encourage others to do so. They participate in public life. They brag about their city—and that, in turn, attracts tourists and prospective residents. They also attract new employers. In an economy based increasingly on providing information and services, rather than producing goods, employers can locate almost anywhere. They will be attracted to cities that provide an outstanding quality of life—and a well-educated workforce.

The public schools are central to my vision for Chicago because I firmly believe that a good quality education is the answer to all the social ills of big cities—crime, poverty, unemployment, economic decline, and middle-class flight. We've worked hard over the past several years to lift student's expectations, to help them see high school graduation not as an end but as a first step toward a successful career in their chosen field. It's not a glamorous endeavor: 85 percent of our public school students come from low-income families that struggle every day with drugs, crime, and, unfortunately, unemployment. You will not read about the strides of the public schools in *U.S. Weekly* or see it on CNN, or in the local daily newspaper, for that matter—at least not regularly. But I believe we should measure our success, at least in part, by the lives we've touched and the horizons we've widened. **Adapted from:** "Delivering Sustainable Communities Summit Address"

For more: www.egov.cityofchicago.org

39.

Be a good neighbor

A great school gives its neighbors a park to hang out in, a goal to aspire to, a building to be proud of, and a standard to maintain.

We worked on a school on Chicago's South Side. It was on the site of an elementary school that had been vacant for 14 years, and had become a real blight on the neighborhood. Chicago Public Schools decided to buy the site and develop a new high school there. The community has a rich African American culture, so the school was named after the African American author Ralph Ellison—he wrote the novel *The Invisible Man* in the 1940s. We thought about how the new building represented Ellison's ideas— that intellectual discovery is a means to freedom. We found a great quote from the book: "I love light. Perhaps you'll think it strange that an invisible man should need light, desire light, love light. But maybe it is exactly because I am invisible. Light confirms my reality; gives birth to my form." We sandblasted it onto the curtain wall at the front of the building. We wanted it to be subtle enough to instill a sense of wonderment and curiosity in the students, and also

big enough to engage the community around the school. It looks like that may be happening— there's a resident of the neighborhood who was very critical of the project initially. Now he says the school is one of the greatest things that's happened in the neighborhood. He's now convinced it's going to produce great leaders.

—Trung Le, OWP/P

WHAT WE LEARNED AT:
OGDEN JUNIOR PUBLIC SCHOOL
TORONTO, CANADA
THE STUDENTS TELL US WHAT SPACES DO AND DON'T
MAKE THEM FEEL GOOD

"The schoolyard is concrete. It's hard and rough and not good to play on. If we put pillows on the playground, that would be better. Then if you fell off the monkey bars you wouldn't get hurt. You could sleep on them too."

"I'd like to write a story under a tree, because it's really quiet and I can focus."

"Red makes me feel bright!"
"I like yellow to match the sun—it makes me feel warm."
"I like black because it's quiet and you can hide."

"I like to be in a small room. It's easier to hear. Also, I'm small so I fit better."

"I like to draw and write in my bedroom on a comfy chair, with my hamster. He smells nice and gives me inspiration."

40.

Build a nest

Children need comfort just as much at school as they do at home. Give them a soft, quiet, and cozy area to play in by themselves or with a few friends.

I have a colleague who gravitated to this idea. She talked about the birds in her garden and how they come back each summer and build a nest in the same beautiful flowerpot. She loves to see how they nurture their young, and believes that's what we should be doing with our young too. We should protect them, and give them the best environment possible.

—Carmen Braun, VS Furniture

CHAPTER 5

SUSTA
SCHOO

The financial benefits of greening schools are about $70 per square foot, more than 20 times as high as the cost of going green.

Traditional schools produce roughly 585,000 pounds more carbon dioxide than green schools.

Conventional roofs need to be replaced 30-50 years earlier than green roofs (with plants in soil on an impermeable membrane), and 20% sooner than highly reflective roofs.

If all new school construction and renovations don't go green, more than $20 billion will be wasted on higher energy usage over the next 10 years alone.

We face a genuine planetary emergency, we cannot just talk about it, we have to act on it, we have to solve it, urgently.

—Al Gore, politician and environmental activist

School buildings represent the largest construction sector in the United States— $80 billion in 2006–2008. Buildings overall are also responsible for 38% of carbon dioxide emissions in the United States, a major contributor to global warming.

Sources (top to bottom): Capital E, *Greening America's Schools: Costs and Benefits*; Ibid; Hashem Akbari Lawrence Berkeley National Laboratory, in Capital E, *Greening America's Schools: Costs and Benefits*; U.S. Green Building Council, "Benefits of Green Schools"; *ABC News,* "Stars join Clinton's campaign to save the world"; U.S. Green Building Council, "Benefits of Green Schools"

In 2001, the average U.S. school district spent $166 per student on energy expenditures.

Schools in the U.S. spend $7.8 billion on energy each year—more than the cost of computers and textbooks combined.

On average, green schools save $100,000 per year—enough to hire two new teachers, buy 200 new computers, or purchase 5,000 new textbooks.

In 2001, 61% of U.S. public school districts reported a shortfall in energy funding.

All education is environmental education. By what is included or excluded we teach students that they are part of or apart from the natural world. —David Orr, environmental educator

Sources (top to bottom): National Center for Education Statistics, U.S. Department of Education, *Effects of Energy Needs and Expenditures on U.S. Public Schools*; National Renewable Energy Laboratory, *High-Performance Schools: Affordable Green Design for K-12 Schools*; U.S. Green Building Council, "Benefits of Green Schools"; National Center for Education Statistics, U.S. Department of Education, *Effects of Energy Needs and Expenditures on U.S. Public Schools*; *In Context*, "What Is Education For?"

In every deliberation, we must consider the impact on the seventh generation ... even if it requires having skin as thick as the bark of the pine.

—Great Law of the Six Nations

Long before Europeans landed in the Americas, the indigenous peoples of the continent had their own systems of governing and decision-making. The six First Nations that inhabited the area now known as the northeastern United States, who were called the Iroquois Confederacy by the French, expected their chiefs to consider three things when making law: the effect of their decision on peace, the effect on the natural world, and the effect on seven generations in the future. Thanks to a revival of interest in the traditions of America's First Nations and a surge of conviction that we must consider environmental impacts, this concept has become an inspiration for the sustainability movement.

We propose it as an inspiration for the sustainable school movement. School buildings contribute a large share of the carbon emissions of the built environment; and yet many are still being operated and built with insufficient attention to the many ways in which, without wise design, they waste energy, dirty the environment, disconnect children from nature, and teach them implicitly that sustainability is just an option, and that disregard for the natural world is permissible.

In this chapter, a chorus of not only environmentalists and sustainability-minded designers but also students, parents, and administrators extol the urgency of sustainable schools. The reasons they give are many: economic, educational, environmental, and moral. As Cayuga Bear Clan Mother Carol Jacobs, a leader of one of the Six Nations, told the United Nations in 1995, "We call the future generations 'the coming faces.' We are told that we can see the faces of the children to come in the rain that is falling, and that we must tread lightly on the earth, for we are walking on the faces of our children yet to come."

DAVID SUZUKI
RECONNECTING SCHOOLS AND NATURE

David Suzuki is an award-winning scientist, environmentalist, and broadcaster and is co-founder of the David Suzuki Foundation, which aims to promote solutions that conserve nature and help achieve sustainability within a generation. Suzuki is also the author of 43 books, including 17 for children, and is renowned for explaining the complexities of the natural sciences in a compelling, easily understood way. He is the recipient of UNESCO's Kalinga Prize for the Popularization of Science and the United Nations Environment Program Medal and is recognized as a world leader in sustainable ecology. He argues here that we must reconnect not only schools but also children with the natural world.

There's a school being built in Essex County, Ontario, that will be Called "Dr. David Suzuki Public School." Why did you agree to give it your name? I spent four years, as a child, in Leamington (Essex County) so I have an attachment. I have been asked to have schools named after me for years and I've turned them all down because I'm not much into leaving monuments to myself. But this one struck me. They are trying to make it into a model green school and since it is in Essex County, I know my mom and dad would have liked that, so I agreed.

They say it's going to be Canada's first school that is LEED Platinum, which is the highest rating of the Leadership in Energy and Environmental Design Green Building Rating System. That's good. All buildings ought to be built to the highest possible LEED standards: it ought to be standard practice. I just feel today's LEED Platinum will be, in the next few years, LEED Bronze.

How much of a watershed do you think a school like this is? I don't think it's a watershed, There are green schools all over the place. For over 10 years now, kids have been writing to me about how they're recycling. When our daughters were in elementary school—[my daughter] Severn's 28 now so this is quite a while ago—we were really upset that their school ground was all concrete and asphalt. We set up a greening committee and planted some organic fruit trees. We had to break holes in the concrete to put them in. But the big thing was that we built a whole series of flower boxes; they were quite large. And we had a day where someone rented one of these little tractors—the kids loved that—and we leveled some hills and rototilled the soil and began our garden. This ought to be what every school child experiences. They're going to spend the bulk of their lives, when they're young, in and around the schoolyard, and yet we have made them into these sterile biological deserts. When we tore up the concrete we found that before they poured it, they had sprayed the schoolyard with pesticides. We had to rehabilitate that soil.

The biggest thing children today need is reconnection with nature. In Canada, over 80 percent of kids are going to grow up in large cities. We live

41.
Leapfrog LEED

Think of today's top rating for environmental school design as tomorrow's last-place rating, and design to be better than the current best practices.

BM: One of the dangers of LEED is that it's a pretty high standard but it's a long way from being where we have to get to.

MW: Some of those standards are relatively easy to meet, though. The fact that you can open a window, for example, is one thing that qualifies.

BM: That's a great idea. It's just kind of ridiculous that it has to be written down!

—Bruce Mau and Michael Waldin, BMD

in a world that is made up of other human beings with a few plants and animals we keep as pets and a few pests that we can't get rid of. I loved insects when I was a boy. It hurts me when I see a kid come in with grasshoppers or ants and the parent's response is: "Take that out of here!" We teach our children to be afraid of or to hate nature.

I read an article where you started out with the question: "Would you let your child play in a swamp?" That was my playground. When I was a kid in Leamington. A swamp. I loved it. Wetlands are among the most biodiverse ecosystems on the planet, but we've treated them as if they are

The most important lesson you learn is that there isn't the environment out there and me in here. The environment is all around us; it's in us.

disgusting, smelly places. We love to drain them and fill them in, and it's tragic because any child who's ever gone out in a swamp will tell you it is a magical place.

How do we reintroduce that magic back into schools? The most magical experience for a lot of kids is to see an egg hatch into a chicken. It's very easy to set up an incubator and have eggs at different stages right in the classroom. For me, the most thrilling experience is watching a Monarch butterfly transform itself into a chrysalis, which is the most beautiful green with gold dots on it, and then see a butterfly hatch. For any child that's ever seen a butterfly emerge from a pupa case, it's one of those life-changing experiences. We need to have those opportunities in the classroom.

The Essex County School Board is talking about having the school building itself become a teaching tool. Well, I think certainly in terms of energy, in terms of waste, there are a lot of lessons that can be learned in that building. But it's crazy to think of a building as separate from its grounds, and where the school is located—Essex County—is devastated in terms of biodiversity. There's nothing left there. It's all farms. During the '70s there were programs for kids to go camping and to do nature things,

but then when the recession hit in the late '80s and '90s they cut what they considered the most frivolous parts of school: sports, nature. I think that we ought to be spending much more money now on field trips—just a day out in the woods, or mucking around with nets. Take the kids to the local ditch. Those are good investments.

Fritjof Capra—he's a scientist who wrote a book called *The Tao of Physics*—founded a place in Berkeley, California, called the Center for Eco-literacy, to try to get kids to realize their part in the ecosystem. He developed a program for K to 12 so that no matter whether it's math or English, there's always an ecological bent to the subject.

Your foundation has developed a curriculum for kids too: The Nature Challenge. Fritjof's is much more extensive; but it's amazing, the minute you give this kind of stuff to teachers they get it right away. It's been very popular among practicing teachers. Can you imagine taking a curriculum like that and adapting it to a school that is purpose-built with sustainability features, as opposed to just trying to make schools that aren't very sustainable, more sustainable!

In your travels to talk to kids, what learning environments have you seen that encourage important ideas about sustainability? There's one school north of Toronto where they were treating all of their sewerage right on site and it was going to plastic pipes that were transparent—you would see this raw stuff going through. I think that's really intriguing. I think that school ought to be a place where you see the world as it really is. And kids like to talk about poop and pee; they're not hung up like their parents. To me the most important lesson you learn is that there isn't the environment out there and me in here. The environment is all around us; it's in us. Sixty percent of our body is water; when you drink water it's come from all over the world. You need food, you take another living creature and make it into your own body. These are very simple lessons, but very profound messages.

42.

Reveal how stuff works

Making school infra-structure literally transparent, to display the flows of water and waste, teaches kids the workings of the real world.

In Europe, in a restaurant, you order fish and what comes to the table is a whole fish with the head still on: It's staring at you! In the United States you rarely get that. I know people that would not eat a whole fish if they saw it. My response is, "Where do you think your dinner comes from?" We've become such wimps; we don't want to see what things really look like.

—Christine DeBrot, VS Furniture

ELEMENTS OF A SUSTAINABLE SCHOOL

THE COLLABORATIVE FOR HIGH-PERFORMANCE SCHOOLS (CHPS) SETS THE BAR FOR SUSTAINABLE FEATURES

Environmentally Responsive Site

To the extent possible, the school's site conserves existing natural areas and restores damaged ones, minimizes storm water runoff, and controls erosion.

Energy Efficient

The heating/ventilating/air-conditioning (HVAC) system uses high-efficiency equipment, is "right sized" for the estimated demands of the facility, and includes controls that boost system performance. The school's lighting system uses high-efficiency lamps and ballasts, optimizes the number of light fixtures in each room, incorporates controls that ensure peak system performance, and successfully integrates electric lighting and daylighting strategies. The walls, floors, roofs, and windows of the school are as energy efficient as is feasible. The building shell integrates and optimizes insulation levels, glazing, shading, thermal mass, air leakage, and light-colored exterior surfaces.

Material Efficient

To the maximum extent possible, the school incorporates materials and products that are durable, nontoxic, derived from sustainable yield processes, high in recycled content, and easily recycled themselves.

Water Efficient

The school uses as little off-site water as possible to meet its needs, controls and reduces water run-off from its site, consumes fresh water as efficiently as possible, and recovers and reuses gray water to the extent feasible.

Easy to Maintain and Operate

Building systems are simple and easy to use. Teachers have control over the temperature and lighting in their classrooms, and are trained how to most effectively use them.

Stimulating Architecture

The school should invoke a sense of pride and be considered a genuine asset for the community.

A Building That Teaches

By incorporating important concepts such as energy, water, and material efficiency, the school becomes a tool to illustrate a wide spectrum of scientific, mathematic, and social issues. Mechanical and lighting equipment and controls can be used to illustrate lessons on energy use and conservation, and daylighting systems can help students understand the daily and yearly movements of the sun.

Adaptable to Changing Needs

The school is able to embrace new technologies and respond to demographic and social changes.

Adapted from: "What is a High Performance High School?"

For more: www.chps.net

43.

Get eco-educated

Before embarking on a program to green a school, learn about what counts the most and what works the best.

When the idea of separating out garbage from recyclables and paper was coming into its own, I had just become the principal of a secondary school with about 1,000 students. The students were super keen on getting blue boxes into the classrooms, and cutting down on garbage. We thought this was an excellent idea, and relatively simple, but we hit an amazing variety of obstacles. Things like: Who would empty the boxes? The union that handled custodial work said they hadn't allocated time in the working day for it. Then, where were we going to store the paper until it was picked up for recycling? At that time, the school didn't have bins, and the district didn't have a contract with a waste removal company. It took us a year to get the system up and running but it was worth it!

—Helen Hirsh Spence, educational consultant to VS Furniture

When you implement sustainable strategies, you become part of a system, and you have to contribute. Chicago rewrote its zoning laws so that with all new buildings, 25 percent of the roof area has to be green roofing. There is no exclusion clause—it applies to non-profits as well as corporations, so even schools are part of this. It means new schools are networked into a matrix of green-roofed buildings, and that matrix has the power to reduce the whole city's heat index on hot days.

—Trung Le, OWP/P

KVERNHUSET JUNIOR HIGH SCHOOL
FREDRIKSTAD, NORWAY
A HIGH SCHOOL MODELS THE SCHOOL BUILDING
AS ENVIRONMENTAL TEACHING TOOL

Kvernhuset Junior High was relocated to a new building on the outskirts of the city within a pine forest and with a granite outcrop as part of the site. The aim was to create both inside and outside space that could be used as teaching tools for environmental studies.

The solution was on three levels. The first level involves making use of existing site qualities: rock, forest, and light filtered through the trees. Places where pine trees were growing on site have been marked inside the building, some tree trunks have been left intact, and the common area is furnished with natural rock formations. Small covered openings in the floor contain various artifacts such as fish and animal skeletons and fragments of stones to attract attention and prompt questions.

The second level makes use of parts of the building to focus on environmental monitoring. Monitoring is divided into three sections: Yellow focuses on solar energy, and has glass-covered construction elements showing the building's insulation. Blue focuses on water, with glass-covered construction elements showing the water pipes. Green focuses on the natural growth and recycling processes, with a roof garden and building elements made of recycled material.

The third level uses features such as a terrarium or aquarium to support ecology studies, as well as posters and pictures of environmental issues in common areas.

The school has proved an effective teaching tool. Pupils themselves show visitors around the school and explain the various features. Designed for secondary school pupils, it offers considerable scope for supporting scientific studies, yet the basic principles are simple and can easily be adapted for use with young children. **Adapted from:** "Bringing the outside inside" **For more:** www.childreninscotland.org.uk

44.

Highlight the site

Every school is located in a particular place with its own unique geological features and natural history. Call attention to a school's site with design, construction, and signage.

KIPP—the network of college-prep schools for under-served communities—was moving into Gary, Indiana, where there's a restoration of a prairie/marshland going on next to the lake. So we put the school there, and made the children stewards. We re-did the curriculum, and the schedules, and the timing based on the ecological timeclock, instead of the human timeclock. So the school, just like the natural world around it, functions differently in winter than in spring, and differently in the spring than in the fall. The children are completely connected to, and participate in, their environment.

—Elva Rubio, BMD

STUDENTS PRAISE GREEN

INTERVIEWS CAPTURE STUDENTS' PRIDE AND
ENGAGEMENT IN THEIR NEW SUSTAINABLE SCHOOL

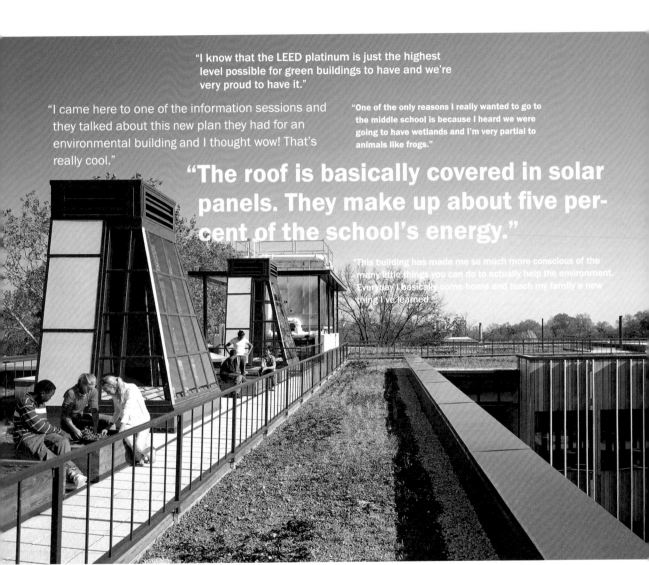

"I know that the LEED platinum is just the highest level possible for green buildings to have and we're very proud to have it."

"I came here to one of the information sessions and they talked about this new plan they had for an environmental building and I thought wow! That's really cool."

"One of the only reasons I really wanted to go to the middle school is because I heard we were going to have wetlands and I'm very partial to animals like frogs."

"The roof is basically covered in solar panels. They make up about five percent of the school's energy."

"This building has made me so much more conscious of the many little things you can do to actually help the environment. Everyday I basically come home and teach my family a new thing I've learned."

Sidwell Friends School is a PK-12, coeducational Quaker day school in Washington, D.C. Guided by its Quaker values, Sidwell Friends is committed as an institution to practicing responsible environmental stewardship. The curriculum is grounded in teaching students about the natural world and their relationship to it. With the decision to construct a new middle school, Sidwell Friends chose sustainable design as a logical expression of its values. **Adapted from:**

—*Generation G Film* **For more:** www.kontentreal.com

45.

Attract like minds

A sustainable school building is a billboard for a school's values and philosophy — it broadcasts the message to compatible parents, students, and staff.

Back in the late 1980s, there was a secondary school on the outskirts of Ottawa that was being designed as the school district's flagship environmental immersion center. The site was near a Class 1 wetland. The project committee that worked on the design included community members, teachers, principals, students, and superintendents. The principal started the process of hiring staff when construction was wrapping up. I went for an interview, and I was grilled, of course, on my experience and on my expertise in my subject area—but

I was also grilled on my environmental ethics and how I lived by them. The principal wanted to make sure his entire staff would be excellent environmental role models for the students, and for the community.

—Helen Hirsh Spence, educational consultant to VS Furniture

DAVID GODRI
A STUDENT-RUN SUSTAINABILITY PROGRAM

David Godri is the director of SWITCH (Solar and Wind Inititatives Towards Change), a non-profit, student-run organization he founded while in high school. SWITCH's aim is to reduce Toronto schools' dependence on the power grid through the generation of renewable energies. Godri was selected as one of the 2008 Youth in Motion's Top 20 Under 20 award recipients and currently attends the University of Toronto in the civil engineering program, where he is pursuing a career in urban environmental sustainability. Godri says founding SWITCH at his high school, William Lyon Mackenzie, was a learning experience on many levels.

William Lyon Mackenzie is a typical high school, with 1,500 kids. In terms of energy, it was pretty low efficiency, because it's really old. It was built in the 1960s. I've always been interested in renewable energy and I started talking to one of my teachers about how to make change. The idea came up to install a few solar panels and a wind turbine on the school. And I just ran with it. Over the summer I put together a proposal. And the first day back at school, I put the proposal on my teacher's desk, and I got a meeting with the principal the next day—at first I thought I was in trouble, but I'm not really a bad student! She was so supportive. And then all the staff came on board. Problem was, the school is owned by the school board, so we had to go through them, and that's a large bureaucracy. I got to the board, and I felt like I was at the UN, because there was an oval of trustees surrounding me and an audience behind, and two massive screens projecting my face. I've always been the shy kid, but I was like: Okay, I just gotta do this because this is what I need to do to get this project going. Then I gave my speech, and the trustee support was amazing.

Students started coming to our SWITCH meetings, staying after school for a good hour and a half, every week. It went from three or four, the first two weeks, to 70 students. I think the reason why so many got involved is because it was a student project. Run by a teacher or the principal, it might not have received the same amount of interest. There was an environmental course offered before we started SWITCH, and only two students signed up for it. Now tons of students have taken that class.

If you have turbines on the school grounds, showing you can generate a lot of power on one school property, students learn how electricity is generated. From turning out the light switch, I didn't completely get it. I started to understand it with the hands-on experience. What I really want to do is have an energy design contest for the most efficient wind turbine. You're teaching not only the curriculum that's necessary—how induction and everything works—you're also teaching the future of what can actually be done. If you have students going home and telling their parents, "We did this at the school, we can do it here," you can expand to residential areas and, before you know it, you have your entire city somewhat run on renewable energies. It's really bringing power generation back to the people who use it.

46.

Let students lead

Hands-on experience is a powerful teacher. Encourage students who want to convert their school to sustainable practices, and let them go for it.

RD: Many schools are developing joint teacher-student committees to look at the effect of their building on the environment.

TL: We are working on a new high school, where the students started a sustainability committee, and asked the physics teacher to join. He happened to be on the design committee for a new school, and offered up the student committee's sustainability expertise.

—Rick Dewar and Trung Le, OWP/P

THE SAVINGS OF GREEN

THE U.S. GOVERNMENT SURVEYS THE NATION AND FINDS
SCHOOLS FROM THE BADLANDS TO THE EVERGLADES
THAT HAVE CUT ENERGY COSTS

The U.S. Department of Energy estimates that utility bills can be reduced by as much as 25 percent if schools adopt readily available, high-performance school design principles and technologies. Even though different climates pose different energy efficiency challenges, schools in a wide range of climates across the U.S. have realized substantial savings in energy expenditures by implementing cost-effective, energy-efficient strategies in their buildings.

Adapted from: *High Performance Schools: Affordable Green Design for K-12 Schools* **For more:** www.nrel.gov

Location: Elk River School District No. 723, MN
Climate: Cold & Humid
Strategies: Large windows for 100% daylighting; ponds for water treatment
Realized Savings: $175,000 a year

Location: **Corvallis School District, OR**
Climate: **Temperate & Mixed**
Strategies: **Energy efficient, digitally controlled lighting, heating, and cooling; Program to turn off computers and lights not in use**
Projected Savings: $1.5 million over five years

Location: Montour School District, PA
Climate: Cool & Humid
Strategy: 10-year Energy Savings Performance Contract with local utility company
Realized Savings: $1.0 million guaranteed by end of contract

Location: Tucson Unified School District, AZ
Climate: Hot & Dry
Strategies: Solar electric system; irrigating with reclaimed water
Projected Savings: $1.0 million a year

Location: Marion County School District, FL
Climate: Hot & Humid
Strategies: Energy accountability program; high-efficiency water fixtures
Realized Savings: $1.0 million over five years

47.

Rally the results

Increasingly, the metrics are out there on the financial benefits of going green. Use the numbers to make the case for an energy efficient school.

For the Chicago Public School system, we did an extensive analysis to see what the cost advantages were of different mechanical systems. CPS decided on a mechanical system that was more costly upfront but also more energy efficient because they were able to recognize the cost benefit. They could project the monetary and energy savings through the 600-plus schools in the CPS system and see a significant payback on an investment that was initially higher.

—Trung Le, OWP/P

CHARLOTTESVILLE WALDORF SCHOOL
CHARLOTTESVILLE, UNITED STATES
A BUILDING CAMPAIGN GREENS A SCHOOL — AND ITS CAMPAIGNERS

The Charlottesville Waldorf Foundation was established in Virginia in 2003 to build a new home for the Charlottesville Waldorf School. By launching a campaign to build "The Greenest School in America"—and demonstrating the fiscal wisdom and pragmatism of doing so—the goal is to teach by example and pave the way for a new movement for sustainability among other schools, corporations, and individuals.

When they first heard about the Greenest School project, parents Marianne Lund and Jim Zuffoletti were in the process of building their own home, and their house became a sort of testing ground for many of the features of the Greenest School project, including low-VOC paint and rain barrels on gutters. Marianne helped develop the foundation's major annual event, the Commonwealth Environmental Leadership Awards (CELA), which honors Virginians who have gone above and beyond in their environmental efforts. "What we learned with CELA," said Marianne, "was the value of this project

to transcend education, to transcend building and to actually create a community around building green." Jim served on the school's board of directors and played a key role on the committee that was instrumental in the construction of Little Green, the first phase of the new building. "I viewed this as a project with incredible leverage. You are talking about a bare bones amount of money on a project that could have tremendous local, regional, and national impact, setting aside the direct implication on our family." That implication, Marianne said, is profound. "I've realized how truly busy we all are, and I think that a lot of the busyness we model for our children isn't busyness of service. It's going to the grocery store, juggling work with home life. Having the opportunity to show my children service to a community is a big deal, and so is having them see that this is a project that is not only important for them but for all the other kids who will be in this school long after they're gone." **Adapted from:** "Commitment to the Power of Two" **For more:** www.greenestschool.org

48.

Do your homework

Many families are trying to shift to more sustainable habits. Aligning the school's goals with those of the families it serves creates a wide community of support for a sustainable school.

BM: Children are carrying the message home. One of the reasons Toronto has been able to do so much with recycling and compost collection is that it used students as a vector. The Toronto District School Board has had a waste minimization program for years, and gives out certifications and awards through its EcoSchools program.

TL: This generation is deeply aware of the global climate crisis. Awareness like that begins with simple acts like my 7-year old son John always wanting to pick up litter because he says he wants to save the Earth.

—Bruce Mau, BMD, and Trung Le, OWP/P

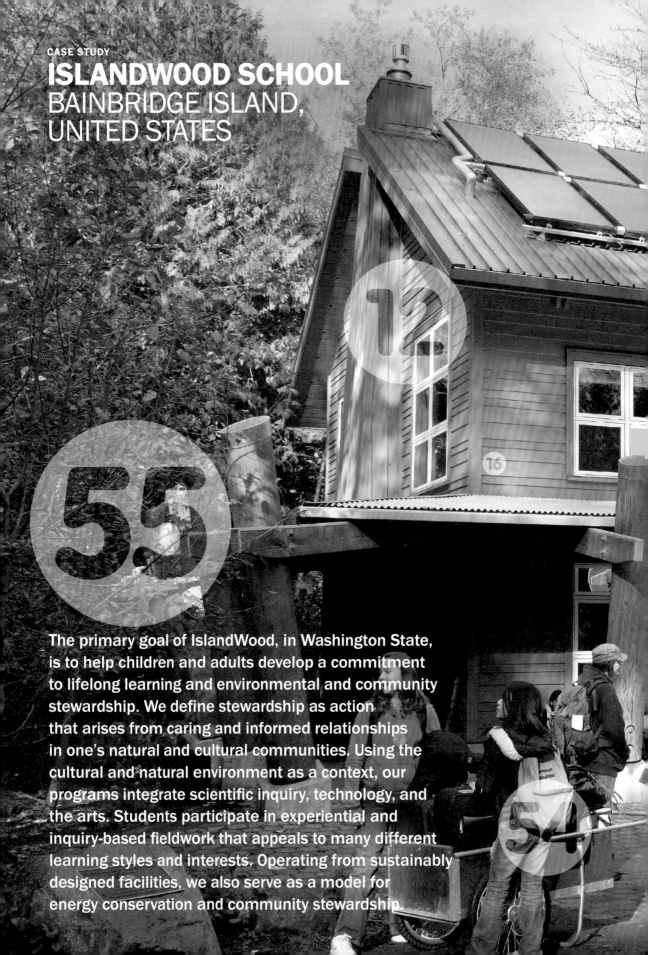

ISLANDWOOD SCHOOL
BAINBRIDGE ISLAND, UNITED STATES

The primary goal of IslandWood, in Washington State, is to help children and adults develop a commitment to lifelong learning and environmental and community stewardship. We define stewardship as action that arises from caring and informed relationships in one's natural and cultural communities. Using the cultural and natural environment as a context, our programs integrate scientific inquiry, technology, and the arts. Students participate in experiential and inquiry-based fieldwork that appeals to many different learning styles and interests. Operating from sustainably designed facilities, we also serve as a model for energy conservation and community stewardship.

A growing body of research links our mental, physical, and spiritual health directly to our association with nature ... As one scientist puts it, we can now assume that just as children need good nutrition and adequate sleep, they may very well need contact with nature.... For decades, environmental educators, conservationists, naturalists, and others have worked, often heroically, to bring more children to nature, usually with inadequate support from policy-makers. Now a number of convergent trends—including intensified awareness of the relationship between human well-being, the ability to learn, and environmental health; concern about child obesity; and media attention to nature-deficit disorder—are bringing the concerns of these veteran advocates before a broader audience. While some may argue that the word "movement" is hyperbole, we do seem to have reached a tipping point. Now comes the greatest challenge: deep, lasting, cultural change.

—*Richard Louv, Last Child in the Woods, www.richardlouv.com*

The inspiration for IslandWood came from the land itself, and the knowledge that half of the Seattle School District's children did not receive overnight outdoor education programs. In 1990, Washington State declared that environmental education was mandatory—yet no funding for teacher training, student programs, or facilities was ever allocated. We learned in 1997 that over a thousand acres of land was being sold on the south end of Bainbridge Island by Port Blakely Tree Farms. Having walked the land and seen the beauty of it, I proposed the idea of a children's outdoor education center. My idea was to take kids out of urban areas and allow them to live in the forest and learn about the natural and cultural history of the Puget Sound region.

Scientists and educators spent time on the property to discern what educational "stories" could be shared with children. Building and landscape architects designed the educational structures, trail system and outdoor field structures, with the help of over 250 children in the fourth, fifth, and sixth grades. The children's ideas focused on adventure-based learning, with their design ideas generating specifics like a floating classroom, suspension bridge, forest canopy structure, and several tree houses.

Now IslandWood provides a complete outdoor classroom with six distinct ecosystems—including a forest, cattail marsh, bog, stream, four-acre pond, and marine estuary.

The buildings are not only places to teach, but are actually teaching elements themselves. The design of our buildings makes it very easy to show what sustainability means in design and construction. We discuss product and material choices and explain why they were chosen. For example, each classroom has a different sustainable floor covering and fixtures: bamboo, cork, recycled tires, and high fly-ash content cement.

On a more abstract level, the operation and theory of many of the spaces allow us to have our visitors think more deeply about their lifestyle and impact on the environment. For example, our buildings have a wider temperature "comfort zone." This means that, at times in the winter, visitors are slightly cooler than in traditional buildings, and in the summer they are warmer. We use these experiences to discuss how wearing a sweater in the winter and shorts in the summer affect energy use through reduced building heating and cooling.

Each building has a solar meadow on the south side that is cut into the woods. The solar meadows are an opportunity to explore seasonal cycles, growth rate of trees, and the cultural history of the site as an old tree farm. The trees removed for the building footprints and solar meadows were milled and used in the buildings, creating another educational aspect to the facilities. **Adapted from:** "IslandWood: A School in the Woods," www.designshare.com and "History of IslandWood" and "What is IslandWood" **For more:** www.newhorizons.org

49.

Get out of the city

Creating places where children can be immersed in the natural world for days or weeks affords learning opportunities that can't be replicated in the concrete jungle.

The Fresh Air Fund has been sending inner-city kids on summer vacations outside urban areas for more than a hundred years. I have a colleague who grew up in Greenwich, Connecticut, and remembers children from Brooklyn spending the summer with Greenwich families. Greenwich is full of parks, and streets with trees—that must have been incredible for those kids.

—Carmen Braun, VS Furniture

WHAT WE LEARNED AT:
ROBERT JUNGK SECONDARY SCHOOL
BERLIN, GERMANY

THE STUDENTS TELL US WHAT THEY NEED TO RELAX
AND RECHARGE AT SCHOOL

"On every table you'll find a plant, and in each corner there are flowers. The curtains and walls are blue to match the color of the sea. This is, for us, an ideal learning environment—both cozy and colorful."

"The most important thing is a sense of harmony between the students and their surroundings."

"Harmonious colors in the class and comfortable furniture for taking breaks."

"I'd like a place in the classroom or the school to chill out and let off some frustration."

"A pleasant place in the corridors and stairs."

50.

Slow the pace

Alcoves and furniture in hallways discourage high-speed traffic and create places of pause.

The renowned Dutch architect of schools, Herman Hertzberger, spent years with behavior scientists and psychologists, and he studied children on his own. One of his most famous designs is the Montessori school in Delft. His architecture is not something that inspires you to say, "It's beautiful," but when you get inside of it and you are around it, you understand it. He really crafted it with the idea of "slowing the pace" in mind. And he did it in a scientific way, not just by intuition or inspiration or personal observation.

—Elva Rubio, BMD

CHAPTER 6

REAL
THE

The typical student's lunch includes chips 5 days a week.

Educational change concerning the significance of the sensory realm is urgently needed to enable us to discover ourselves as complete physical and mental beings... an unbiased and full understanding of human existence is a prerequisite for dignified life. —Juhani Pallasmaa, architect

There are about 100 touch receptors in each of your fingertips.

All people have the instinct to decorate their surroundings.
—from *A Pattern Language*

Color is the most immediate form of non-verbal communication. We naturally react to color as we have evolved with a certain understanding of it, partly because the survival of our ancestors depended on it with regard to what to consume and avoid.
—from *Colour: Basics Design*

Sources (top to bottom): Feed Me Better, *Killer Facts About Our Weight Problem*; *Educational Philosophy and Theory,* "Embodied Experience and Sensory Thought"; Oracle Education Foundation, ThinkQuest, "Come to Your Senses: Your Sense of Touch"; Christopher Alexander, *A Pattern Language*; Gavin Ambrose and Paul Harris, *Colour: Basics Design*

The average person has about 10,000 taste buds and they're replaced every 2 weeks or so.

Things before words, concrete before abstract.

—Johann Pestalozzi, pedagogue and educational reformer

Study has found that 75% of learning occurs through visual stimulus, while 13% occurs through hearing and touching. Smell and taste counts for 12%.

The mind's first step to self-awareness must be through the body.

—Dr. George Sheehan, runner and author

There are 16,000 hair cells, or sound receptors, in a human cochlea.

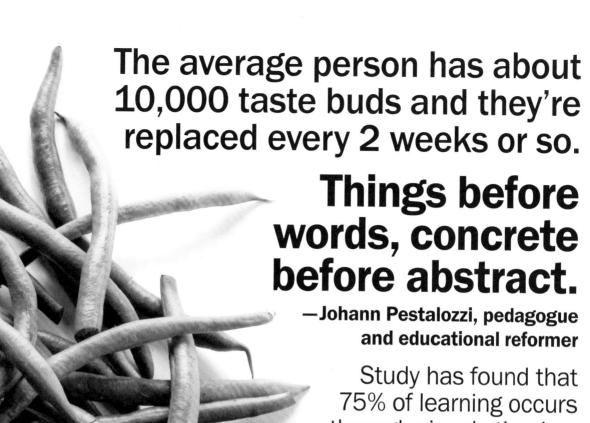

Sources (top to bottom): KidsHealth, "What Are Taste Buds?"; Norman Brosterman, *Inventing Kindergarten*; Qais Faryadi, UiTM Malaysia, "The Montessori Paradigm of Learning: So What?"; *Think Exist*, "George Sheehan"; The Howard Hughes Medical Institute, *Seeing, Hearing, and Smelling the World*

We are instruments endowed with feeling and memory. Our senses are so many keys that are struck by the nature that surrounds us and that often strike themselves.

—Denis Diderot

It came to be called the Age of Enlightenment, the era of reason and rationalism, when philosophers and intellectuals such as Denis Diderot and his compatriot, the seminal thinker on education Jean-Jacques Rousseau, were questioning traditional institutions and assumptions. One of the works that established Diderot as an original thinker was called *Letter on the Blind*, in which he argued that a person depended on his senses to develop his ideas. Diderot made his argument by examining the case of the blind who, he proposed, could be taught using the senses they still possessed, notably touch.

Diderot's ideas were too enlightened for his contemporaries, and his essay earned him a three-month stay in prison. Two and a half centuries later, the belief that we develop our intellect through our senses is unlikely to land its adherents in jail, but it is still a radical idea in most learning environments. While we allow preschoolers to use their bodies, their hands, their noses, their ears and sometimes even their tongues to explore their worlds, by primary school most students are sentenced to spend their school days in settings that are either bland or chaotic, settings where little thought has been given to sensory education. Concrete schoolyards, locker-lined corridors, fluorescent-lit classrooms, cacophonous cafeterias where kids would rather lob french fries than eat them—no wonder schools turn out students who are over-stimulated and under-sensitized.

The senses, the contributors to this chapter argue, are the gateway to the mind, particularly the developing mind. School cooks, parents, educators and designers demonstrate how, from the kitchen to the schoolyard, the auditorium to the library, there are myriad opportunities to integrate food, light, color, and material into the learning landscape and create teaching moments that will resonate with students on a visceral level. It is high time that we built schools reflecting Diderot's 260-year-old insight that our environments orchestrate our senses.

ANN COOPER
REVIVING SCHOOL KITCHENS AND STUDENT TASTE BUDS

Ann Cooper is the director of nutrition services for the Berkeley Unified School District and is the former executive chef and director of wellness and nutrition of the Ross School in East Hampton, New York. There, she cultivated an innovative food program serving regional, organic, seasonal, and sustainable meals. Former executive chef of the Putney Inn in Vermont, Cooper is a graduate of the Culinary Institute of America. She is the author of many books, including *Lunch Lessons: Changing the Way We Feed Our Children*. Here she raises a battle cry for vegetable gardens, home cooking, and dining rooms in all schools and uncovers how they came to be seen as luxuries rather than necessities.

You call yourself "the renegade lunch lady." Who were America's original lunch ladies? I don't know for sure, but I'm assuming they were moms who figured it was a way to pick up a little extra money and be home when the kids got home from school. They weren't professional cooks—they were moms who cooked, and the food was mom kind of food.

The kitchens they were working in—what would they have been like? We're talking the beginnings of the National School Lunch Program, about 60 years ago. Imagine kitchens of the '40s and '50s—we've all seen pictures of them.

In contrast, can you talk about what you found when you arrived for the first time, in 2005, at the Berkeley Unified School District kitchen? They had one central kitchen that was a mess. It had no stove. It did have two ovens, and some refrigerators. There was a can crusher for all the empty cans, and a box cutter to open all the frozen boxes. But there really wasn't food. Like most schools, they stopped cooking 25 or 30 years ago, and everything that came in was processed or frozen.

What did this environment say to you about the role of food and eating in schools? That nobody gives a shit! Maybe that's a little too strong. What happened was that the School Lunch Program started because there weren't enough physically fit recruits for World War II. The reason the recruits weren't fit is that they were malnourished. The government realized they needed to feed kids better in schools so they could fight in the war. And, with the best intentions, the government was also trying to support farmers. Segue to 25 years later: The lunch ladies and all the equipment were on their last legs—both ready to retire. Schools didn't have the money to reinvest in educating new lunch ladies or putting in new equipment. This was at the same time as refrigeration was becoming ubiquitous, and as the rise of processed foods. So the big processed food companies said, "Hey, you don't need equipment or trained staff. Here, you can have chicken nuggets." And that's what started the downfall. We were a country enamored with technology and processed foods. The schools were just looking at it from the bottom-line standpoint: "It's easier, it's safer, it's cheaper." What we lost sight of is that kids

51.
Make caterers caretakers

Consider the people who prepare school meals, and the places where those meals are prepared and served, critical to children's well-being—and hire and

were at the other end of this, consuming it. And now here we are, 30 years later, with an obesity crisis and a diabetes crisis. That's the outcome.

How have you transformed what you found when you started at the Berkeley Unified School District kitchen two and a half years ago? Well, the kitchen isn't much different. I added a steamer and two slow-cook ovens. But we've changed all the food. It's all "scratch cooking," no more processed foods at all. And we are remodeling, and building a new central kitchen. Most kids haven't been in the old kitchen, but in the new one, they get to see everything. It'll be an open kitchen.

> The kids grow food, they taste it out of the garden, they're learning where food comes from.

You came to school cooking from a career as a chef in high-end restaurants; your first school cooking job was at the Ross School, a private school in New York State. The students there eat in something called the Wellness Center. Can you describe that environment? It's a three-story building. There's a basement level, where there are showers and lockers. The main level is a really big gym and some offices. And then the top level is the cafeteria. It looks more like a restaurant than anything else. It's really beautiful, with a lot of artwork, a lot of bamboo, a lot of glass.

How did the kids behave in that kind of environment? Perfect! There was no outside food allowed on campus. Everybody ate in the cafeterias—faculty, staff, students, administration—multigenerations sat down and ate together. There was never a food fight, never any pushing. When you expect kids to behave, by and large they do.

When we adults go out to a fine-dining restaurant, we're encouraged to experience the food on our plates in a multi-sensory way—the texture, the smell, the sound of the crunch, and so on. Is it important to introduce that concept to school children? We have hands-on experiential cooking and gardening classes in almost all our Berkeley Unified schools. You can't overestimate the value of

that—for the reasons you just mentioned. So, yes, it's really important. The kids grow food, they taste it out of the garden, they're learning where food comes from.

Earlier, you mentioned the bottom line. Let's talk about the economics of school lunches. The National School Lunch Program reimburses schools $2.49 per child per day. Of that, two-thirds typically goes to payroll and one-third to food. So, most schools are spending 80 to 90 cents on food—you just can't do healthy food for that. The National School Lunch Program spends tax dollars—$8 billion a year—to feed 30 million children a day. Well, we're spending $200 billion a year on diet-related illness now, and only 10 or 11 percent of our kids have Type 2 diabetes. The Center for Disease Control says that one out of every three Caucasians and one out of every two African Americans and Hispanics born in the year 2000 are going to have diabetes in their lifetime, most before they graduate high school. So we're talking about 40 to 45 percent of all school-age children having diabetes within 10 years. Two hundred billion dollars is going to become $400, $600 billion. I talk about how that $8 million we spend on school lunches needs to double, and people say, "Where are we going to get that?"

Why do you think people have difficulty wrapping their heads around the idea that tasty, nutritious, home-cooked food is something that all children should have in school? Because there's so much money in the "bad food" system. Big corporations spend $20 billion a year advertising non-nutrient foods to children. It's not that people don't want better food for kids. We almost need to have an uprising, a huge grassroots effort that says, "Our kids need to come first. Big business and its profits can't be more important than our kids."

52.

Spend now, save later

Equipping school kitchens and making wholesome lunches can be costly, but the lifelong health impacts of a poor childhood diet are even more expensive.

THE EDIBLE SCHOOLYARD

ONE OF AMERICA'S MOST BELOVED CHEFS
REVEALS HER MISSION TO EDUCATE THE SENSES
OF CHILDREN AS WELL AS ADULTS

SCHOOL FOOD HERO

A BRITISH PARENT AND GARDENER WIELDS FLOWERS
AND PLANTS AS TOOLS AGAINST VANDALISM
AND APATHY

Over 30 years ago, Alice Waters began a revolution for organic food when she opened her restaurant, Chez Panisse, in Berkeley, California, and, for the past decade, this former Montessori teacher has attempted to integrate nutrition and education. In 1994, she created the Edible Schoolyard, a program at Berkeley's Martin Luther King Jr. Middle School where students work in a one-acre organic garden on school grounds, in a kitchen classroom, and in the cafeteria, preparing and serving the food they'll eat for lunch. In 2004, Waters persuaded the Berkeley Unified School District to adopt a curriculum integrating food into almost every aspect of the school day. It's a very holistic way of educating, she says, a very Montessori way. "I use all of my Montessori principles in everything that I've done—in the way I run my restaurant, the way I've conceived of the program in the Berkeley schools. It is all deeply based on education of the senses. I think helping people to open up their senses is a wonderful way to really reach them. Getting them to smell and taste, and to really see things." **Adapted from:** "An Interview with Alice Waters" **For more:** www.amshq.org

A low-income housing project gardener who gave up his free time to help set up an after-school gardening club at his local primary school near Bradford (United Kingdom) was named the first national "food hero" in the U.K. Soil Association's annual school food awards, which recognize and celebrate an individual who has worked hard to make a difference in school meals in their area.

Steve Thorpe, who has two daughters at the school, Howarth Primary, initially set up the gardening club as a way of resolving some vandalism problems in the town. Flowers and plants were grown and used to smarten up the town center, and the vandalism stopped. The project has gone from strength to strength, and now 40 members of the club (another 20 eager pupils are on a waiting list) plant and tend vegetables, while the whole school gets involved in harvesting the vegetables, shelling peas and peeling potatoes in the school kitchen, then eating their efforts for their school lunches. Thorpe has earmarked the thousand-pound prize the school wins to pay for a much-needed extension of the school greenhouse. **Adapted from:** "Local volunteer transforms pupil's attitudes to vegetables in a successful school gardening club" **For more:** www.foodforlife.org.uk

53.

Grow your own

Growing and preparing fruit and vegetables on school grounds educates children's senses of taste, touch, and smell.

Richard Louv, who wrote the book *Last Child in the Woods*, coined the term "nature deficit disorder"— that's when kids have been so abstracted from nature that they can't relate to life in a full way. I experienced it working as a canoeing instructor with kids who lived only in an urban context: If you asked them when a tomato grows, they'd tell you a tomato grows all the time because it's available all the time. They didn't have any knowledge of the cycles and rhythms that are only really accessible in the context of natural growth and life.

—Bruce Mau, BMD

THE TACTILE BODY
THE BRAIN'S SKIN-SENSATION MAP DEMONSTRATES THAT
THE SENSE OF TOUCH IS A POWERFUL LEARNING TOOL

You have a pretty good idea of what you look like from staring into the mirror each morning. But your body's appearance is radically different from the way your brain perceives it, because the sensory nerves in your skin that send messages to the brain are more densely packed in some areas than in others. For example, the touch sensors in a single fingertip are 15 times more numerous than those on the legs, so the area of the cerebrum— the somatosensory cortex—representing one finger is much larger than that representing a leg. This means that the brain's skin-sensation map, called the homunculus, or "little person," looks weird. **Adapted from:** "How Your Brain Sees You"

For more: discovermagazine.com

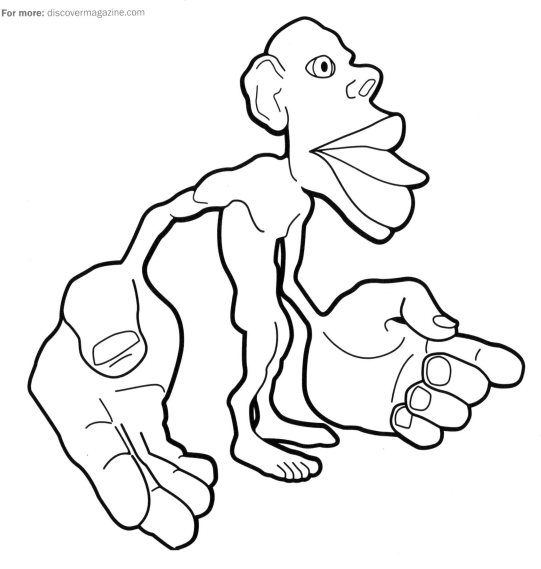

54.
Think hands-on

Children of all ages need places where they can learn by touching, manipulating, and making things with their hands.

I was reading a book called *Orbiting the Giant Hairball*. The introduction talks about someone giving a lecture to school children. He's talking about art, and he asks first-graders to raise their hands if they're an artist. And the whole class raises their hand. And then he asks the second graders: 70 percent of them raise their hands. He goes on to the third graders, and fourth graders, etc. And by the time he gets to sixth grade, only three people raise their hand. It's shocking how quickly kids lose the ability to consider art a central behavior.

—Monica Bueno, BMD

I went to school in an agricultural community in Michigan, and we had a school farm, with chickens, and cows—everybody learned how to milk a cow!

—Christine DeBrot, VS Furniture

INTERVIEW
JUHANI PALLASMAA
ALLOWING CHILDREN TO BE ROOTED IN REAL LIFE

Juhani Pallasmaa has practiced architecture since the early 1960s. In 1983, he established his own office, Juhani Pallasmaa Architects, in Helsinki, Finland. In addition to architectural design, he has been active in urban, product, and graphic design and has taught and lectured all over the world. He has published books and essays on the philosophy and critique of architecture and the arts. One of his best-known and most influential works is *The Eyes of the Skin: Architecture and the Senses*. He argues that schools these days, like most buildings, fail to feed any of the senses except sight and, in so doing, cut off learning from life.

By and large, we live in a visual world. The tactile ingredient in vision has disappeared. There are many reasons behind that; one reason is that the visual world is instant, whereas the tactile world is very slow. The visual world is public, whereas the tactile world is always intimate. I have written critical analyses of this visual bias; now, in recent years, I have been thinking about the integration of the senses. For instance, when you look at a Matisse painting, say an interior with a balcony door opening onto a harbor on the Mediterranean, you begin to feel the moist warmth, hear the sounds of the harbor, and smell the plants. In the industrialized western world, sight has taken over to a degree that it is the only socially acceptable sense. I'm interested in how vision can be enriched by accepting these other sensory realms.

I am in a group of Finnish psychologists, educators, editors, who are trying to change curriculum-driven attitudes toward education and consider the whole human person as the starting point, and the role of sensory experience in the human constitution. There are all kinds of sensory experiences that are essential material for compiling an understanding of yourself, of the world, and these do not have to be designed in a very meticulous manner.

For instance, I can still smell my first day at school 65 years ago. This was during the war years; I had been brought from the city, where we lived, to my grandfather's in the Finnish countryside. I went to a rather simple school there, but it was a sophisticated education in some ways. In those days, students in a farming community took turns going to school at 6:30 in the morning, before the other students came at 8:30, to put on a fire in the stove to heat up the schoolhouse. In retrospect, I appreciate those dark mornings in the chilly school building. It created a sense that school was not just an abstract place for learning; it was integrated with life. The smell of burnt wood and of the soap by which the wooden floor was washed: those smells are very much the essence of school for me. There has to be a smell of life in a healthy environment. My school experience has a strong taste element too, because in those days we all brought our own sandwiches, and in the war years meat was scarce, so it was dry bread with butter and sliced tomatoes. I love still that taste.

Tastes and smells can be landmarks of orientation and memory. We are better off and our learning skills are improved if we are strongly rooted in our settings. Let children be rooted in real life. Rooting means safety, and safety allows mental space for learning.

55.

Trigger the senses

Sound, smell, taste, touch, and movement power memory. An environment rich in sensory experiences helps students retain and retrieve what they learn.

Dr. Breithecker, who is interviewed in chapter three, says there's a great exercise for the vestibular system or sense of balance: standing on one foot. He tells us we should do our crossword puzzles that way. Better yet, stand on one foot and close your eyes. Of course, then you have to put down your crossword puzzle!

—Dr. Axel Haberer, VS Furniture

CREATING A WORKSHOP FOR THE SENSES

A DESIGNER PROVIDES GUIDELINES FOR
ENVIRONMENTS THAT ACTIVATE CHILDREN'S SENSES

Children are a laboratory for the senses, with each sense activating other senses. They have a synaesthesic capacity: they "see" temperature, they "touch" light, they "taste" smells. The childhood environment constitutes an enormous workshop of the senses and is an integral part of learning and an active element in it. It is difficult to design flexible, changeable spaces that are continually altering and, simultaneously, to provide these places with an identity. Design processes that have been found most useful make use of color, light, sound, and smell. The image of the space is derived from the sensory richness of its material.

Color

Use a subtle chromatic range with many shades. Include colors similar to each other, tone upon tone, which can generate vigor and variety, and colors that contrast with one another.

Light

Offer an environment illuminated from a variety of sources: incandescent, fluorescent, vapor, halogen, etc. Light should be able to create shadows. Provide concentrated as well as diffuse light and different color "temperatures": warm white, cool white, rose white. Staff and children should be able to vary the light intensity and color.

Materials

Create a multi-sensory setting with surfaces that are smooth and rough, wet and dry, opaque, bright, translucent, and transparent. Have features that change over time (wood, stone, flowers, fabrics) or remain unchanged (glass, steel).

Adapted from: "Space to play, room to grow"
For more: www.childreninscotland.org.uk

56.

Design in multiple dimensions

Evaluate ideas, features, and materials for the learning environment on their sensitivity to color, light, and texture.

We were invited to speak at a conference at the Loris Malaguzzi Foundation in Reggio Emilia, Italy—the conference was called Pedagogy and Architecture in Dialogue. And we got a chance to see the Reggio Emilia schools. They're specifically geared toward multiple senses. Water is a big part of the learning environment—it's not perceived as being messy. Inside the classroom, they set up water experiments. And light experiments. They took an old overhead projector—the kind people don't use anymore—and the kids put marbles, glass tiles, anything transparent on it and projected amazing shadow patterns. The kids are creating their own unique environment to interact with.

—Trung Le, OWP/P

WHAT COLOR FOR WHAT ROOM

A PAINT PRODUCER DETAILS THE WAYS IN WHICH
COLOR CAN ENHANCE—OR INTERFERE WITH—
THE FUNCTION OF A SCHOOL SPACE

Color has the power to influence a facility's atmosphere and the performance of its occupants. Where you specify bright, attention-getting colors and mild, calming colors depends a lot on the function of the space.

In classrooms, students and educators need to feel stimulated and motivated, but not so much so that the colors discourage concentration. An effective technique is to paint the teaching wall a deeper or brighter shade than is used on the side walls. This does two things: It attracts attention to the front of the classroom, yet the eyes get a visual break when focus is shifted to the side walls.

Libraries don't need to be dreary, dull spaces. Actually, using color to warm and brighten these spaces encourages students to read. Walls and shelves lined with books can be energized with the use of colorful wall graphics. Frequently, libraries also contain computers, so remember to select colors that help reduce glare and eyestrain in these areas.

Auditoriums, gymnasiums, and cafeterias are often poorly lit. In addition, their large size makes color selection a critical issue—bright colors on large expanses can easily overwhelm the space. Lighter warm tones or neutrals are recommended for the main color, with brightly colored accents to invigorate the room.

Corridors and stairwells are ideal spaces for bright, happy colors to reflect school spirit. Lockers can be painted school colors. Mascots and other colorful wall graphics add interest. Strategic use of appropriate colors can help visually shorten long hallways and enlarge small, dark ones. In corridors and stairwells, combinations of colors also can be used effectively to color code sections of the building—depending on use, for example—and can aid navigation and traffic flow in a large or multistory building. **Adapted from:** "Light and Color Goes to School"

For more: www2.peterli.com/cpm

57.

Paint by function

Determine what each space in a school is used for, then specify a paint color that supports the mood of the space.

When we did our design workshop for this book with students in Berlin, the kids said one of the things they really wanted in their learning environment was color—they absolutely craved it. But they didn't want just any colors, they wanted natural colors: the greens of grass and trees, and the blues of the ocean and the sky. If there was one consistent idea that came out with all four classes we worked with, it was this need for natural colors—and for natural light.

—Helen Hirsh Spence, education consultant to VS Furniture

THE CHILD'S EXPANDING WORLD
A RESEARCHER READS CHILDREN'S MAPS FOR CLUES ABOUT
THE LEARNING LANDSCAPES THEY NEED

Rebecca, 5 years old

Mathew, 7 years old

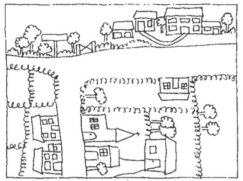

Heather, 9 years old

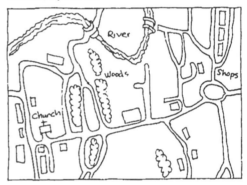

Travis, 11 years old

Analyzing neighborhood maps collected from hundreds of children in the United States, England, and the Caribbean, and doing interviews and field trips with these same children, has produced clear patterns of development in the relationship between the child and his or her expanding world.

From ages four to seven, children's homes fill the center of their maps, and much of their play is within sight or earshot of the home. Children often describe the worms, chipmunks, and pigeons that live in their yards or on their blocks, and they feel protective of these creatures.

From 8 to 11, children's geographical ranges expand rapidly. Their maps push off the edge of the page, and they often need to attach extra pieces of paper to map the new terrain they are investigating. Children's homes become small, inconsequential, and often move to the periphery of the map. The central focus in their maps is the "explorable landscape."

From ages 12 to 15, the maps continue to expand in scope and become more abstract, but the favored places often move out of the woods and into town. Social gathering places such as the mall, the downtown luncheonette, and the town park take on new significance.

At each of these stages, children desire immersion, solitude, and interaction in a close, knowable world. We take children away from these strength-giving landscapes when we ask them to deal with distant ecosystems and environmental problems. Rather, we should be attempting to engage children more deeply in knowing the flora, fauna, and character of their own local places. The woods behind the school and the neighborhood streets and stores are the places to start. **Adapted from:** "Beyond Ecophobia"

For more: www.orionmagazine.org

58.

Define the learning landscape

A child's world expands as he develops. Keep pace by providing environmental experiences that are developmentally appropriate.

HELLERUP SCHOOL
HELLERUP, DENMARK

In the late 1990s, the municipality of Gentofte, in Denmark, projected that its population of children would double in the coming years. Gentofte embarked on a comprehensive school development and expansion program to refurbish 10 old schools and build one new one, Hellerup School. Gentofte used the transformation of its schools' physical environments as an opportunity to develop a new program of teaching and content, influenced by the theory that all children learn differently, some by seeing things, others by hearing, and yet others by movement or touch.

In Denmark, the Act on Educational Environment for Pupils and Students was introduced in 2001. In this act it is written that all pupils and students have the right to a good educational environment in order for the teaching to take place in a way that is both healthy and safe. The educational environment must improve the participants' opportunities for development and learning. Therefore, the act also includes the physical and aesthetic environment of the educational establishment.

In an interview in the book *Aesthetic, Yes Please*, the instructor Jens Arentsen says: "We have to ask ourselves: Why does the body like to be in some places and not other places? Why do we emotionally like to be in some places? Let's find the answer to those questions. And then try to organize the school and classrooms accordingly."

Architects collect knowledge and experience about how the room stimulates children and young people, about how materials, rhythm, textural effects, and light influence our well-being. Within the past 10 years, studies have been made of the development of the brain and the senses, and we now know much more about what it takes to create a good learning room.

—Ulla Kjaervang, "Power of Aesthetics to Improve Student Learning," www.designshare.com

To reach the main entrance of Hellerup School, you walk through a special educational landscape featuring vegetation that winds its way across the schoolyard, small paved bumps that are painted in strong contrasting colors, and a pool with stepping stones. Arriving at the school proper, you take off your shoes and contribute to the landscape of footwear that both students and teachers establish every day when they change into slippers or socks for school. You feel an immediate difference, one that triggers your sensory apparatus. Without shoes, you have discarded a shield against reality: You are closer to the floor, and you can feel your feet in a different way. Without shoes, you feel at home. In this way, the first step inside Hellerup School is an awareness-raising process in which you prepare mentally for school through the physical changes—now I step into the universe of the school, now my senses are ready for learning.

Once inside and without shoes, you arrive at a large staircase in an atrium, a room that serves as the school's center and heart. Here you find stairs that are much more than a way to get from floor to floor. A great variety of activities happen on the stairs: movement, sitting, education, teamwork, presentation, and recreation—the stairs are seating for film screenings. Many students also have their lunch on the stairs. The staircase creates a flexible space that can be used in numerous, diversified learning situations. It also activates many senses by demanding action—do you want to go up or down,

jump or stop, sit or stand—and in that way enables children to make choices and become more aware of their bodies.

The interior of Hellerup school is dominated by wood: the staircase, balconies, and panels around the building. The wood creates a warm atmosphere, which, together with the slippers, helps provide calm and tranquillity. Wood is also a tactile material that speaks to the senses. There is a big difference between sitting on a concrete staircase and sitting on a wooden staircase.

Teaching mainly takes place in the students' home areas, which are located in more quiet corners. The home areas are the children's base for everyday school life; they are a more organic replacement of the traditional school structure of permanent classrooms. Designed as large, open areas—from 330 to 400 square meters—with space for several classes, they can be subdivided with mobile shelves and display walls. The layout can be specified to match the students' age, and classes can, to a large extent, rule over their home areas and make them their own. At Hellerup School, contemporary forms of learning and physical organization fit together like two parts of the same story. **Adapted from:** *Without shoes, without inhibitions—ready for learning* **For more:** www.arkitema.com

59.

Slip off your shoes

Creating a learning space that's safe and comfortable to navigate in socked or slippered feet offers an opportunity to use a physical act— the taking off of shoes —as mental preparation for learning.

WHAT WE LEARNED AT:
CHICAGO ACADEMY FOR THE ARTS
CHICAGO, UNITED STATES

THE STUDENTS TELL US WHAT IT FEELS LIKE TO
BE WELCOMED AND CONNECTED BY SCHOOL

"I spent my first two years of high
school in a monstrously big public
school, and I read a lot of fiction in
those two years. Once I came here, I
started reading a lot more nonfiction
—biographies, history books. What I
realized was that, in my first two years,
I was trying to escape the academic
environment I'd been thrown into."

"Community involvement is so
important—it gives people an
opportunity to see what we're doing,
and it makes us feel safer too."

"I once saw a school in Japan where all the
classrooms were joined—no corridors, just glass
walls that open onto other spaces. That way, no
one's afraid to walk down the hallway—it's a totally
open environment."

"When I think about the kind of space
I would want to learn in, I imagine
open windows, natural light, and a
comfortable chair to sit in."

"It's cool being surrounded by art. I realize there's
so much in common between different fields. I feel
like I'm more in tune with how connected everything
is—both academic and non-academic."

60

Open the doors

Give students places to exhibit their work as if it were in a public gallery, then invite the public to come and have a look.

A.E. Stevenson High School in Lincolnshire, Illinois, has integrated artwork into the entire school building—two- and three-dimensional artwork. There are galleries off the main circulation space just for displaying student artwork. The school's developed a program for buying the best student works. This happens every year. The students get a small sum, their work goes on permanent display, and they learn that it has value, not only to them but also to people who experience it. The program is modest, but it gives students the recognition and self-confidence they need to develop their creative talents.

—Rick Dewar, OWP/P

CHAPTER 7

LE

FOR

75% of America's six million students with disabilities are being educated in the general education classroom.

In 2000, over 200,000 students in federally funded programs had some form of physical impairment, such as deafness, blindness, or multiple impairments.

An estimated six million children in the U.S. have a disability that makes it hard or impossible for them to play on traditional playgrounds.

In 2005–06, about a third of African American students and a third of Hispanic students attended high-poverty schools compared with 4% of white students.

Research has demonstrated that the cost of accessibility is generally less than 1% of total construction costs; however, the cost of making adaptations after a building is completed is far greater.

In low-income communities, only 50% of students graduate from high school. On average, those who do graduate read at an eighth grade level.

The vast majority of children with disabilities have moderate impairments that are often not visible or easily diagnosed. Disabled children include those with learning difficulties, speech difficulties, physical, cognitive, sensory and emotional difficulties.

Sources (top to bottom): National Education Association, *NEA Report on the Individual's with Disabilities Education Act*, in National Clearinghouse for Educational Facilities, *Creating Accessible Schools*; U.S. Department of Education, *The Digest of Educational Statistics, 2001*, in Microsoft in Education, *Accessible Technology: A Guide for Educators*; National Center for Boundless Playgrounds, "About Us"; National Center for Education Statistics, *Findings From The Condition of Education 2008: Enrollment, Student Diversity on the Rise*; The World Bank, *Education for All: The Cost of Accessibility*; National Assessment of Educational Progress, in Teach For America, "Our nation's greatest injustice"; The World Bank, *Education for All: Including Children with Disabilities*

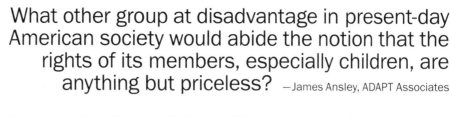

What other group at disadvantage in present-day American society would abide the notion that the rights of its members, especially children, are anything but priceless? —James Ansley, ADAPT Associates

Educational disparities unfairly limit the life prospects of the 13 million children growing up in poverty today, impacting their earning potential, voter participation, civic engagement, and community involvement. Moreover, these disparities disproportionately impact African American, Latino/Hispanic, and Native American children, who are three times as likely to live in a low-income area.

In the United States, nearly one in five Americans has some level of disability. In Canada, it is one in six.

I do not accept an America where we do nothing about six million students who are reading below their grade level—an America where 60% of African American fourth graders aren't even reading at the basic level. —Barack Obama, president of the United States

When I was a boy on the Mississippi River there was a proposition in a township there to discontinue public schools because they were too expensive. An old farmer spoke up and said if they stopped building the schools they would not save anything, because every time a school was closed a jail had to be built. —Mark Twain, author

Fourth graders growing up in low-income communities are already three grade levels behind their peers in high-income communities.

Sources (top to bottom): National Clearinghouse for Educational Facilities, *Creating Accessible Schools*; National Center for Children in Poverty, in Teach For America, "Our nation's greatest injustice"; Microsoft in Education, *Accessible Technology: A Guide for Educators*; Obama for America, "Remarks of Senator Barack Obama: Our Kids, Our Future"; Mark Twain, *When in Doubt, Tell the Truth: And Other Quotations from Mark Twain*; National Assessment of Educational Progress, in Teach For America, "Our nation's greatest injustice"

Knowledge is the most democratic source of power.

—Alvin Toffler

On what he called "the edge of the 21st century," futurist Alvin Toffler wrote *PowerShift*, the final volume in the trilogy he began with his influential bestseller *Future Shock*. In *Future Shock* and the books that followed, he predicted that to prepare for the future we must change our understanding of the present and the trajectory into which it propels us. *PowerShift* focuses on power, which, Toffler argues, remains one of the least understood and most important aspects of our public and private lives. Toffler writes that of all sources of power, knowledge is fundamentally different because it can be grasped by not only the rich and the strong, but also the poor and the weak.

That conviction underlies Toffler's vision of the places we dedicate to knowledge—schools. He describes his school of tomorrow as open 24 hours a day; students, who would begin their formalized schooling at various ages depending on their individual preparation, would arrive at different times of day. Toffler's vision is of a place fully accessible to all learners, regardless of their individual characteristics—and in that it is, sadly, a truly futuristic vision. Many of today's schools are inaccessible to students who are physically, emotionally, intellectually, socially, or economically challenged, and that puts knowledge, the supposedly most democratic source of power, beyond the grasp of the weakest and poorest citizens of what we call the developed world.

The good news is that, as we see in this chapter, a broad cohort of educators, scientists, researchers, lawyers, designers, and philanthropists share Toffler's vision and have concrete ideas for how we can and must design learning environments that are not only accessible but welcoming. The thinkers gathered here urge us to address pragmatic and humane changes, and push us to think beyond, to the changes that will make a learning environment the kind of vibrant and engaging place that truly puts knowledge within the grasp of all.

NÍNIVE CALEGARI
PURVEYOR OF PEG LEGS, EYE PATCHES, AND HOMEWORK HELP

Nínive Calegari is the cofounder of the San Francisco children's writing center 826 Valencia and is now serving as the CEO of 826 National. She is a veteran public school teacher with 10 years of classroom experience. Before teaching in her family's hometown in Mexico, Nínive Calegari worked at Leadership High School, San Francisco's first charter school, where she also served on the Board of Directors. She is coauthor of *Teachers Have It Easy: the Big Sacrifices and Small Salaries of America's Teachers* and the recipient of the George Lucas Educational Foundation's Edutopia 2007 Daring Dozen award. She is a passionate advocate for overworked teachers, at-risk students, and environments that make learning accessible by making it fun.

Before cofounding 826 Valencia, you were a public school teacher. Why did you want to help create a learning environment outside of the school system? I'm not an anti-school, anti-institution person. I was excited to support teachers from the outside because, having been in the schools, I know how stressed they are. Their schedule is so draining, and the number of students is so tremendous, that it's hard to do dream projects. So I was happy to participate in any opportunity to bolster teachers and be a connection with the community. The founding site is in the Mission District in San Francisco, which is a primarily Latino and Mexican American community.

Why did you chose to launch there? I feel connected, being Mexican American myself. It's easy for me to relate to the families—I share their culture. And the Latino community is having a devastating time with graduation rates—only 25 percent of Latinos graduate from high school. I feel incredibly proud of Latino culture, and I want to make sure that school institutions are effective and that there are bridges to the immigrant community. 826 can

provide that bridge, whether it's through homework help or going into schools, or making sure that student work is being published.

You aim to help a range of kids—from those who are aspiring writers, to those who want help with writing-related homework, to those who are English-language learners. Why is it important for 826 to reach kids at, as your website says, every opportunity? If there is something that we can do for somebody, we would like to do it. Young people who are aspiring writers are inspiring, and we want them to have avenues to meet people who are making a living from writing. And yet we try to put the bulk of our resources into kids who wouldn't otherwise have that opportunity. So, the tone and the culture of our place is very friendly but, because we do have limited resources, behind the scenes when we're deciding which schools to go into, we're looking at which schools have the most low-income kids, who are not getting as much extra support or special projects. We have flocks of tutors that go into the schools and work during the school hours. Tutoring happens—I wouldn't say day-and-night, but day-and-

61.

Adopt a young mentor

Allow someone younger than you to become your advisor on hopes and dreams, and let those aspirations become inspirations for learning environments.

OWP/P participates in Chicago's ACE Mentor Program. It's an annual program that takes local high school students through a design project. The students get to work with young architectural professionals, solving real-life problems in an actual office environment—some of the kids have never been in an office before. And the young professionals are energized by the experience of working with the students. The mentors gain as much as the people they're mentoring.

—Rick Dewar, OWP/P

afternoon-and-evening, for sure. We'll be anywhere that a child is willing to meet us—literally.

826 Valencia takes its name from the address of the storefront that it occupies in the Mission District—and you run an actual store there. It's a pirate store, and it's fun, and funny, and welcoming.

What would someone coming into the store see? It has beautiful wood drawers along one side—crazy, mismatched shapes. In every drawer you're going to find different pirate supplies that you may need. In the floor there are trapdoors, and mops fall from the ceiling. There are gorgeous antique signs everywhere that are framed and have jokes in them. You can find peg-legs, glass eyeballs, little handmade books that describe how to take care of your eyeballs. You'll see a ton of professionally made student publications, and books, and magazines, and maps, and pirate shirts and pirate socks. Everything you need if you're an aspiring pirate.

The play is a tool to get to the hard work, but it doesn't mean that there isn't hard work.

How do the kids respond to the store? A little bit of shock and then smiles. There's an immediate sense of warmth and playfulness that's apparent to all age groups. If you're seven, you may like digging through this big sand vat for treasures, which you can barter for a poem or a story. If you're 15, you might start digging into some of the signs on the wall and reading the jokes. If you're 35 or 75, you may enjoy picking up the books and magazines. What's cool about the store—and this is true for all the stores around the country—is that there are entry points for each group. At the New York 826, for example, because it's a superhero store, there's a cape trying-on machine. You put on a cape, and you step onto this platform, and they turn on a fan and you can see if the cape has good aerodynamics given your shape. All the stores are beautiful in different ways, and all so unlike an institutional place. This is not a remedial center. There isn't a sense of, "Oh, I have to go to my bummer tutoring center because I'm behind in school work." The stores and their wackiness influence the atmosphere and the culture of the whole place.

So there isn't a hard line between the store and the tutoring center—here's the fun stuff and now here's the serious stuff? There's no hard emotional or symbolic line. There is a gate or a door, because you can't have strangers coming back when the kids are there. There is a serious line in that the goal is that your homework is done, and that it's completed well, and that you've comprehended it—and that's serious. But it's done in a joyful way, with tutors and kids who feel proud of their work at the end of the day. The play is a tool to get to the hard work, but it doesn't mean that there isn't hard work.

You mentioned the superhero store, in New York. 826 National now has writing centers in a total of seven American cities, and the store seems to have become an integral part of the concept. Why? There's a couple of reasons. The stores actually make money, and that's important because foundations and other investors appreciate it when you have multiple sources of income. And the other thing that's interesting: in the Mission, there are a ton of non-profits but we're one of the only ones with an open door. So the store is important as a financial tool, and it's also incredibly important as an outreach tool. There are thousands of people who just walk by and pop in: "Ooh, what is this? Maybe I'll buy a leather-bound diary," and then, "Wow, you're tutoring students! Maybe I'll become a volunteer," or "Oh, I have a friend who knows somebody who is a foundation officer." There's a hundred connections that happen in any given afternoon. That's why the stores are on walking streets.

Bearing in mind the limited resources of public schools, how can they replicate or at least emulate the tone of 826? Having been a public school teacher, I know it's hard when you have 146 or maybe 172 students, and your schedule is demanding. I would get so tired that I would forget about the joy of learning. I don't know that 826 can help people remember the joy, but if schools and communities can figure out ways to partner, and remember that we all actually feel good when we learn something, that the "a-ha" is fun—that, I think, will inspire kids.

62.

Put the fun in fundamentals

Injecting a learning space with playfulness and humor creates a warm and welcoming atmosphere.

This goes back to Abraham Maslow's Hierarchy of Needs that we looked at in chapter one: If children feel safe, they are ready to learn, and if they are having fun, they feel safe.

—*Carmen Braun, VS Furniture*

Lego holds an international competition to build robots out of of Lego blocks—VS Europe is a partner. It is a great project, because from this playful activity, children are also learning about engineering, computer science, and teamwork.

—*Dr. Axel Haberer, VS Furniture*

CONTEXT
EVERY BRAIN IS DIFFERENT
THE CENTER FOR APPLIED SPECIAL TECHNOLOGY'S
IMAGES OF BRAINS AT WORK ILLUSTRATE THAT
EVERYONE FUNCTIONS DIFFERENTLY

CONCEPT
UNIVERSAL DESIGN AND UNIVERSAL DESIGN FOR LEARNING
TWO ORGANIZATIONS REWRITE THE WAY ACCESSIBILITY
IS DESCRIBED AND DESIGNED

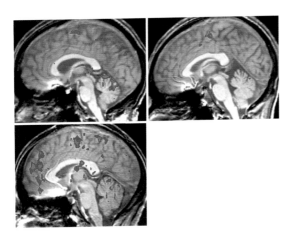

These three functional magnetic resonance images show brain activity patterns of three different people performing the same simple, finger tapping task. The level of brain activity during performance of this task is designated using color. Blue indicates a low to moderate level of activity, red indicates a high level of activity, and yellow indicates an extremely high level of activity. Each of these three individuals shows a unique pattern of brain activation.

Adapted from: "Brain Imaging Showing Individual Differences"

For more: www.cast.org

Universal design is not a fad or a trend but an enduring design approach that originates from the belief that the broad range of human ability is ordinary, not special. Universal design accommodates people with disabilities, older people, children, and others who are non-average, in a way that benefits all users. After all, stereo equipment labels that can be read by someone with low vision are easier for everyone to read; public telephones in noisy locations that have volume controls are easier for everyone to hear; and building entrances without stairs assist equally someone who moves furniture, pushes a baby stroller, or uses a wheelchair.

Universal Design for Learning embraces the concept of improved access for everyone and applies it to curriculum materials and teaching methods. A teacher's goal is for every student to learn skills and understand the subject, but not every child learns in the same way. Traditional curriculum materials tend to offer only limited flexibility for meeting that goal. Universally designed curriculum overcomes limitations by incorporating three principles of flexibility into the design: multiple methods of presentation, multiple options for participation, and multiple means of expression. This built-in flexibility provides a wider range of options for students to choose from—meaning the curriculum adapts to the student, rather than the other way around.

Adapted from: "About Universal Design"

For more: www.udeducation.org

63.

Design with words

What you say influences what you think and what you do. Use the term universal design, rather than accessible design, as a reminder of what it's all about: creating an environment for all learners.

Let's have a global dialogue about how we can help children with special needs learn. If we truly believe that we all learn differently, and that there's been proven success with the individualized education model, then we can replace the label "special needs design" with "universal design." For example, the "small learning community" model allows special needs children to be mainstreamed, and learning environments with a variety of spaces that support a variety of learning modes and styles can support special needs as well.

—*Trung Le, OWP/P*

INCLUDING STUDENTS WITH DISABILITIES

RESEARCHERS SAY STUDENTS WITH DISABILITIES SPOT BARRIERS AND COME UP WITH SOLUTIONS OTHERS DON'T

INCLUDING DESIGNERS WITH DISABILITIES

AN ADVOCACY ORGANIZATION FORWARDS THE ARGUMENT THAT NO ONE IS BETTER EQUIPPED TO DESIGN FOR DIVERSITY THAN DESIGNERS WITH DISABILITIES

Facilitating inclusive school environments requires ensuring physical access, affording the opportunity for optimal learning and social experiences, and providing a nurturing climate. Without these elements in place, students with disabilities are denied an equitable educational experience.

However, what is lacking are empirically based studies where the barriers to inclusion and full participation in general school settings are identified by those most impacted—students with disabilities. Even in a school designed to remove architectural barriers for students with severe physical disabilities, 83 percent of the students reported unmet accommodation needs.

Therefore, we examined barriers and facilitators to accessibility and inclusion within eight different school settings based on comments from students with physical disabilities and their parents. The students in these eight schools were fully capable of identifying and expressing both barriers and facilitators to inclusive school environments. In fact, we asked them only about structural and attitudinal barriers, and they extended the task to include unintentional attitudinal barriers and ethos considerations, as well as policy and procedure issues. They identified four kinds of improvement required: modifying physical structures to improve accessibility, addressing negative attitudes through increased disability awareness programs, dealing with the lack of knowledge or understanding through increased inclusive education of teachers and staff, and, finally, developing more inclusive education policies. Students should be allowed and encouraged to participate in evaluating inclusive environments. **Adapted from:** "Barriers and facilitators to inclusive education as reported by students with physical disabilities and their parents" **For more:** www.questia.com

The disability rights mantra of the 1990s applies to the design industry today more than ever: "Nothing About Us Without Us" is a slogan that implores policy- and other decision-makers to include the people most directly affected by design decisions in solving their own problems and creating better opportunities for everyone's benefit. But why is this necessary?

Only people with disabilities can pass on understanding about our lives, our feelings, our wants and desires. We have seen the power of the personal history within various cultures, in the practice of African Americans, persons of Hispanic origin, and women. Our non-disabled families and friends, and the professionals who try to help us, can empathize with our lives and often contribute, but they cannot merge design knowledge with disability understanding in an intuitive way.

When designers with disabilities participate in the planning and design of housing, landscapes, workplaces, and schools, we gain a combination of personal experience of disability and professional design skills. When that happens, pluralism in functional use of structures and products isn't an afterthought; it is integrated into the fundamentals of design and subsequent use. And, aesthetically, our pluralistic world needs new challenges and new ideas that incorporate beauty with function. These solutions to accommodate diversity might possibly come slowly from educated non-disabled designers, but the process will be more elegant and coherent when designers with disabilities are involved from the start. **Adapted from:** *Building a World Fit For People: Designers with Disabilities at Work*

For more: www.adaptiveenvironments.org

64.

Recruit difference

The brightest way to arrive at inventive solutions for a pluralistic learning environment is to build diversity into the design team.

We like to think about a sports team as a model: To be successful, a team needs individuals with a variety of personalities and skill sets, each contributing their particular strengths.

—Carmen Braun, VS Furniture

FEATURES OF AN INCLUSIVE PLAY ENVIRONMENT

A GUIDE TO OUTDOOR PLAY ENVIRONMENTS DECLARES
THAT ACCESS HAS MANY FEATURES

The key features of an inclusive play environment are: person-accessible, activity-based, sensory-rich, developmentally appropriate, and flexible.

Person access:

Beyond simply planning for full wheelchair access, person-access requires thoughtful consideration of children who are visually impaired, hearing impaired, cognitively delayed or impaired, have speech impairments, are shy, have low balance, have reduced fine motor and/or gross motor control, etc.

Some questions that may be asked when developing or choosing play activities would be:

Does the play setting allow the child to use their means of playing independently?

Does the activity have a tactile element as well as a visual difference?

Does the wheel, knob or lever allow for manipulation without grasping?

Does the activity encourage two or more players?

Activity based:

The traditional approach has been to ensure that there is a variety of equipment—slides, swings, climbing frames, etc. These pieces of equipment, although they look very different, promote only one type of activity. A play area should promote a variety of types of activities, rather than fill an equipment list. Each type of play activity meets a number of distinct developmental needs: dizziness activities, passive resting, exploratory activities, dramatic activities, interactive activities, and practice activities.

Sensory rich:

Organized sensory elements assist children in understanding the play environment. For example, a tree may be audibly marked with a wind chime; raised Mayer-Johnson symbols on equipment may provide visual and tactile clues as to its use, and an active portion of the play area may have a "red" theme, while a "quiet place" may be more green.

Developmentally appropriate and flexible:

While timing and the rate of development may vary, all children need to develop in five crucial areas for proper growth: social/emotional, intellectual, sensory, perceptual/motor, and physical. The particular needs of children and the type of stimulation necessarily change according to the developmental stage of the child. Play environments must be powerful enough to sustain the child's interest and motivation without constant motivational and/or directional assistance from an adult. **Adapted from:** *Inclusive Outdoor Learning Environments: an introductory guide* **For more:** www.beyondaccess.org

65.

Get accessibility aware

There's more to access-
ibility than meets the
eye. Making a learning
environment truly inclusive
means designing from
multiple developmental
perspectives.

At Northside College Preparatory High School in
Chicago, we solved the problem of how to make
a school stage accessible to all kids who want to
perform. The only way to enter most stages is
from backstage, whereas at Northside we designed
a walkway that wraps around the audience.

—Trung Le, OWP/P

HIGH POINT SCHOOL
ANN ARBOR, UNITED STATES
TWO NON-PROFIT ORGANIZATIONS PROVIDE THE
MEANS FOR COMMUNITIES TO BUILD ACCESSIBLE
PLAYGROUNDS, AND NEW UNDERSTANDINGS

"It's during play that children learn to take turns, make decisions, make friends," says Amy Jaffe Barzach, cofounder and co-executive director for the National Center for Boundless Playgrounds. "It's essential that kids with disabilities get a chance to play too, otherwise they're doubly disadvantaged." Boundless Playgrounds was established in 1997. As one of the Kellogg Foundation's 75th Anniversary grantees, the organization's Able to Play project is helping 20 Michigan communities build barrier-free playgrounds.

An Able to Play project brings entire towns together to contribute time, expertise, and enthusiasm. Families, landscape architects, park officials, and builders collaborate from day one to play, design, raise funds, and of course, build. The Michigan sites receive assistance from Boundless Playgrounds, beginning with strategic planning that includes adults and children with and without disabilities.

Jan Culbertson, a project coordinator at High Point School, Ann Arbor, Michigan, was particularly grati-
fied at the participation of the school's students. "The kids all wanted to be involved, and they worked incredibly hard, designing T-shirts, doing fundraising," says Culbertson. "One of the manufacturers didn't allow anyone under 18 to build, so the kids kept busy seeding and mulching while adults were doing the structure."

The rewards from undertaking an Able to Play project went far beyond the job site, says Culbertson. "You build a whole community by doing something like this," she says. The national Boundless Playgrounds team agrees that their projects tend to become a focal point for both children's play and community change. "The more that communities work with people and with children of all abilities," says Leslyn Odom Clark, Boundless Playgrounds director of corporate relations, "the more we'll see all kinds of barriers disappear." **Adapted from:**
"No Barriers to Fun, Friendship on Boundless Playgrounds"
For more: www.wkkf.org

66.

Break down social barriers

The process, as well as the outcome, of building an accessible playground can bridge all sorts of community divides.

VICTORIA BERGSASEL
SCHOOLS WHERE ALL STUDENTS ACHIEVE

Victoria Bergsagel founded and directs Architects of Achievement, a network that helps communities across the country integrate the work of facility design into school reform. Harvard-educated, Victoria has been a high school teacher, counselor, principal, district administrator, and adjunct professor. She now serves as a consultant, featured speaker, and design jurist for clients ranging from school districts to national architectural organizations to education departments in the United States and abroad. Much of her work focuses on designing schools where achievement is accessible to all students.

We have an educational crisis in the United States: Only 70 percent of our students graduate from high school. There's a variety of reasons why we lose kids. The American education system, especially the curriculum, is a mile wide and an inch deep. We think kids need to be exposed to a lot of things, but the result is they're never fully engaged in anything. So some kids who drop out are smart—they just become bored. Some kids are getting in trouble because they're being asked to sit still and behave themselves, and for whatever reason they're not. Some kids have go to work to support their family; in some of the urban areas there's the presence of unhealthy influences. I spend time working in Los Angeles, where they have a huge gang problem. Los Angeles has high schools approaching 5,000 students—that's very impersonal. A gang addresses a basic human need for belonging. So how can schools create a sense of belonging? How can they help kids stay connected? Kids are natural explorers—how do we maintain their sense of wonder and curiosity?

Our schools should look more like our high-functioning industries do. I have a friend in the biotech industry who says, "There are times when I'm in my lab, nose-to-the-grindstone, eyes-on-the-microscope, trying to solve a problem with my research. I go up to get a cup of coffee, and I'm standing there at the cafe table with somebody, talking about what

I'm trying to solve, and all of a sudden it'll hit me." So we need to design a variety of different spaces in schools, and provide for informal as well as formal learning spaces. We want kids so excited about their learning that as they spill out of that classroom they may still be talking about it. Rather than spilling out of classrooms with desks lined up in rows into a very institutional hallway, they could find everything from soft seating and conversation nooks to working conference tables. We're trying to make learning a more vibrant activity, more accessible to all students, and make schools joyful places to learn.

67.

Make it feel good

Schools that are engaging, vibrant, great places to be foster a sense of belonging that's important for all kids, especially those at risk.

In Germany, when I was in school, the class pretty much owned the classroom and the teachers came and went. So we stayed in the same room every day for every class and it was not very nice—pretty dull, the walls were all white. Our class got together and we went to the principal and said "We want color in the classroom!" And so they allowed us to paint our walls. We did all different shades of yellow and orange, and everybody was allowed to do some creative thing on the wall. It was great, because all of a sudden this made the classroom much more our own.

—Carmen Braun, VS Furniture

BUILDING SCHOOLS FOR THE LEARNING GENERATION

RICHARD RILEY, FORMER U.S. SECRETARY OF EDUCATION,
LINKS AMERICA'S FUTURE TO ITS SCHOOLS

Our schools and colleges have always given us an edge as world leaders. Now our secret is out and the rest of the world is making massive investments in their schools. We are in a global education race to the future.

So while Alan Greenspan worries about the nation's GNP—our Gross National Product—I worry about our country's GIP—our Gross Intellectual Product—the brain power and creative genius we need to drive biotechnology and all the new knowledge industries yet to be dreamed.

Unfortunately, many of the trend lines in our nation's Gross Intellectual Product are headed in the wrong direction. Data from the Trends in International Mathematics and Science Study tell us pretty clearly that we are losing ground to our foreign counterparts, even though America's students start school on an equal footing. Indeed, by the time they reach high school, a third of our students have dropped out—1.2 million students a year. In many low-income schools, the graduation rate is less than 50 percent.

Tom Friedman, the author of the best seller *The World Is Flat*, makes the point that when baby boomers were growing up, their parents used to tell them to finish their supper because children in India were going hungry. Now, baby boomers are telling their children to finish their education because children in India are hungry for their jobs.

John Stanford, the late superintendent of schools in Seattle, used to say, "The victory is in the classroom." His mantra is my mantra today.

Organizing our schools for success can only happen if we really think differently about how our schools are built and how they function. Creating smaller learning environments is one smart way to help teachers do their job. We seem to be making progress on that score. But there is still much more that has to be done.

Today's teachers and children have one foot in the future and the other in the past. The Internet, cell phones, text messaging, MP3 players, are ubiquitous in the lives of our children. They often spend hours working with their friends to conquer the intricacies of complex games. Their daily activities foreshadow their future work. But too often when our children walk into their schools, they step into the past, as they enter isolated classrooms to sit behind desks that their parents and grandparents would recognize.

The Learning Generation needs access to a broad range of 21st-century learning opportunities that cross the boundaries of home, school, and work. They need schools that challenge them to develop the information, communication, thinking, and collaborative problem solving abilities that will lead to success in a rapidly changing world. We also need to build schools in new ways as well. We are spending about $30 billion a year to build new schools and many of these schools are being built for 1950 instead of 2050.

In this era of lifelong learning, the young people who make up this new Learning Generation need to be able to go back to school again and again to keep on learning. This why we need to move away from the old factory model facility and build schools that are truly 21st-century community learning centers. **Adapted from:** "Creating America's First Learning Generation" **For more:** www.nctaf.org/documents/Riley.05Symp.pdf

68.
Take it to the top

Politicians can create a climate of support for new schools that are accessible to all learners. Lobby them to think about Gross Intellectual Product as well as Gross National Product.

I get tired of the money discussion. We need to give education much higher priority. Here in the U.S., we're taking our global standing for granted, while the rest of the world is not only catching up—they're leap-frogging past us.

—Trung Le, OWP/P

VELBERT SCHOOL FOR EDUCATIONAL SUPPORT AND COUNSELING
VELBERT, GERMANY

In Germany, Schools for Educational Support and Counseling, known as E-schools, mentor pupils who do not receive adequate care and support from their families or conventional schools. Mettman, a county in North Rhine-Westphalia, Germany, has been the first to build an E-School, in the town of Velbert, that aims to be exemplary in terms of both pedagogy and architecture. Given the constraints on budgets for public school building, the design was also optimized to be economical, and in that way to serve as a model for the integration of architecture, pedagogy, and cost-effectiveness.

The concept of "children with special educational needs" extends beyond those who may be included in handi-capped categories to cover those who are failing in school for a wide variety of other reasons that are known to be likely to impede a child's optimal progress.

The degree to which an individual pupil may be considered as having a handicap must be viewed as emanating from many different sources. It must be especially emphasized that the school environ-ment may play a central role in the transformation of individual characteristics into handicaps. The general approach must be that every pupil be seen as potentially able and creative. The school is responsible for creating environments where this potentiality can develop.

—"Quality Indicators" and "Special Needs Education" www.unesco.org

The design imperative for the Velbert School for Educational Support and Counseling was to create a school environment that gives teachers, pupils, and parents confidence, identity, and a sense of belonging.

Over a period of four years, the architects (Roland Dorn with Roland Bondzio), together with building administrators, educational officials, school directors, consultants, teachers, and students, collected suggestions, re-examined conventional guidelines, and explored a variety of new paths. The conception, form, and design of the school was developed to be a teaching aid in the guise of a building. It aims to promote the communication of rules for living, rather than conventional subject matter.

From the main entrance loggia on the ground floor, the central element of the school is visible: its "forum." Flooded with daylight, this forum translates the topography of the sloping site into a hall that has the character of an amphitheater; its circular shape hints at the form of the complex as a whole. All the remaining rooms are located in a ring around this central space. The forum aids communication and enhances student orientation; its glass roof allows ample light to reach not only the floor but also the galleries, and a glazed passage provides access to the garden and views onto the beech forest beyond. By acting as a meeting point and a multifunctional area, the forum lives up to its name.

In contrast, the classrooms and group-work rooms are designed to provide calm and allow their occupants to concentrate. On each of the school's two floors, there are three pairs of classrooms sharing an entrance. Each pair of classrooms has its own color scheme; the decor of these rooms is intended to convey the feel of a family dwelling. Each classroom unit consists of a large instruction room and a small group-work room: the latter is of equal importance because group activities are an opportunity for students to learn how to ameliorate conflicts and practice alternative behavior patterns. The classroom units have pantry kitchens and cooking is taught as a way to promote cooperation and minimize aggression. Elements that encourage tidiness, such as cloakrooms, sideboards, and built-in cupboards, are of particular importance in the day-to-day work of this school, since they contribute to the atmosphere of emotional commitment. The circular layout of the building can be detected in every room. All the shapes, materials, lighting and colors in the school have been chosen to convey a tranquil ambiance and support the pedagogical approach. **Adapted from:** "Lebens und Lernraum Schule"
For more: www.montag-stiftungen.com

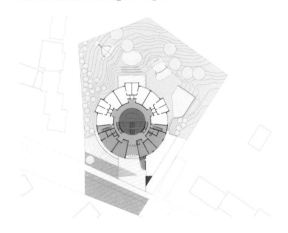

69.

Domesticate classrooms

Equipping learning spaces with domestic features such as kitchens, pantries, and cupboards can help make a school feel like a home.

In the Cayman Islands high schools, featured in chapter two, we wanted to shift away from the "cells and bells model," where you move when the bell rings, eat when the bell rings. We introduced a cafe into each of the four academies, so the students can take a break and go get a snack when they are hungry or thirsty, rather than when the bell rings.

—Trung Le, OWP/P

WHAT WE LEARNED AT:
THE LONDON DESIGN DINNER
LONDON, UNITED KINGDOM

THE PROFESSIONALS TELL US WHY WE NEED TO LISTEN
TO THE STUDENTS AND INITIATE CHANGE IN OUR SCHOOLS

Peter Brown, educational consultant, The School Collaborative | Ty Goddard, director, British Council for School Environments | Stephen Heppell, CEO, heppell.net | Gareth Long, educational consultant | Helen Hirsh Spence, educational consultant | Shelagh Wright, associate, Demos | Dr. Thomas Müller, director, VS Moebel | Richard Dewar, principal, OWP/P | Trung Le, principal, OWP/P

A lot of ideas we are discussing here have been around since 1900. Of course, society is different today and we have new challenges, but we're still asking ourselves how we can build the best learning environment for our children. —Dr. Thomas Müller

A lot of people forget the students. Very few people ask them anything. Students know how they like to learn. And they learn when they're not in school. —Gareth Long

Humanity in schools is sometimes missing because educators are focused on delivering set curricula. What needs to be designed into schools is time allocation for teachers to connect individually with students and other colleagues. It would mean greater collegiality and collaboration. —Helen Hirsh Spence

We need to understand "campaign" in a 21st-century sense of the word. It's not a campaign that we are in control of. The only way to make a campaign work is to give it away. We must give it away. —Shelagh Wright

What we've forgotten, in our pursuit of ideas, is good old campaigning and getting political. We've got to start shaping a movement that has global implications. Give me a plan of action—I crave action! Teachers in the classroom crave action. What we've done too often is swap stories—we need to do that; it's very human. But now we need to get to a different page. —Ty Goddard

The first point is to recognize that the sytems, in various degrees, are failing. —Trung Le

The economy has changed rapidly. There are no more jobs for mindless people, and the biggest industry on the world stage is learning. But schools deliver compliance, uniformity, obedience, punctuality, and not much else. It won't be the end of the world if schools don't make it—but it would be the end of the world if learning didn't make it. —Dr. Stephen Heppell

70.
Create a movement

Engage in meaningful conversations about changing the education landscape. Parents, teachers, students, principals, community members, and politicians are all important and powerful stakeholders in this movement.

CHAPTER 8

REW

LEAR

Roughly 60% of American teenagers own a cell phone and spend an average of an hour a day talking on them—about the same amount of time the average teenager spends doing homework.

8–18 year olds spend on average 6 hours and 15 minutes per day in front of screen media (computer, TV, video games, etc.), and only 43 minutes in front of print media.

95% of surveyed students in the EU aged 12 to 18 years have their own mobile phones.

32% of all teens do not use the Internet at school at all, despite the fact that 99% of public schools have access to the Internet.

In the U.S., 46% of tweens use mobile phones.

The majority of principals reported that less than 25% of their teachers had the technical skills necessary for engaging students in using ICT effectively.

47% of teen bloggers write outside of school for personal reasons several times a week or more compared to 33% of teens without blogs.

The vast majority of teens and their parents believe that use of the Internet helps students in the classroom and in their studies.

Sources (top to bottom): PEW Internet & American Life Project, Teens and Technology; The Henry J. Kaiser Family Foundation, Generation M: Media in the Lives of 8-18 Year-olds; Mediappro, with the support of the European Commisssion, Safer Internet Action Plan, The Appropriation of New Media by Youth; National Center for Education Statistics, Digest of Education Statistics, in PEW Internet & American Life Project: The Internet at School; Nielsen Mobile, "46% of U.S. Tweens Use a Cell Phone, Nielsen Reports"; Statistics Canada, Education Indicators in Canada: Report of the Pan-Canadian Education Indicators Program 2005; PEW Internet & American Life Project, Writing, Technology and Teens; PEW Internet & American Life Project: The Internet at School

Teen use of the Internet at school has grown 45% since 2000.

Where the computer's true power as an educational medium lies – in the ability to facilitate and extend children's awesome natural ability and drive to construct, hypothesize, explore, experiment, evaluate, draw conclusions —in short to learn—all by themselves. —Seymour Papert, educator and technology expert

87% of U.S. teens aged 12–17, or 21 million youth, use the Internet.

78% of online teens (16 million) say they have used IM to talk about homework, tests, or schoolwork.

57% of teens online are "content creators," building web pages for themselves and their friends or for a school assignment or an organization.

The quantity of information doubles every eight years. This means by the time a child born today graduates from college, the amount of knowledge in the world will be four times as much, and by the time that child is fifty it will be thirty-two times as great. By then, ninety-seven per cent of everything known will have been learnt since that child was born. —Alvin Toffler, author and futurist

31% of 8–18-year-olds have a desktop computer in their bedroom and 12% have their own laptop.

Sources (top to bottom): PEW Internet & American Life Project, *The Internet at School*; Seymour Papert interviewed by Dan Schwartz, "Ghost in the Machine: Seymour Papert on How Computers Fundamentally Change the Way Kids Learn"; PEW Internet & American Life Project, *Teens and Technology*; PEW Internet & American Life Project: *The Internet at School*; Edutopia, The George Lucas Educational Foundation, "12 Million: Teen Content Creators"; Alvin Toffler, *Future Shock*; The Henry J. Kaiser Family Foundation, *Generation M: Media in the Lives of 8–18 Year-olds*

It is tempting, if the only tool you have is a hammer, to treat every-thing as if it were a nail.

—Abraham Maslow

We began our book with Basic Needs, a chapter whose title is inspired by Abraham Maslow's pioneering work on what people, including children, need to survive and thrive. We are ending with a chapter introduced by his contention that the tools we have influence the knowledge we obtain. Maslow was a pioneering scientist who began his career studying the behavior of dogs and monkeys and made his mark exploring the psychological processes of human beings. These processes, he explained in a book of memoirs, did not fit into "the extant machinery for achieving reliable knowledge." By machinery, Maslow meant the scientific methods and concepts of the 1930s, and he clinched this observation with his hammer-and-nail remark.

For those of us who grew up before personal computers and electronic aids became ubiquitous, when the tools for learning were pencils and spiral-bound notebooks, chalk and blackboards, it is tempting to treat learning as a purely mental activity, and technology in the schools as a toy, a frill, or a distraction. For those of us scrambling to keep up with the Information Age, it is tempting to dismiss machine shops and hands-on skills as outdated and unnecessary. This hammer-and-nail thinking is flattening our schools: Too many of them have dismantled workshops and studios, yet have installed little in their place except already obsolete computer labs.

The child who starts kindergarten this fall may not know how to spell her name, but she will know how to surf the Web. The engineers, entrepreneurs, educators, researchers, and school administrators whose stories conclude this book make a compelling case that learning itself is already rewired, and that we must create learning environments as flexible and fluid as today's technologically sophisticated learners. All we can know about the world that today's kindergarten student will step into when she graduates is that it will have, to paraphrase Maslow, machinery for gaining knowledge beyond what we can imagine.

JAMES DYSON
INNOVATION HIGH

James Dyson studied at the Royal College of Art, where he developed an interest in design and engineering. Upon graduating, he joined engineering company Rotork and developed the Sea Truck, a high-speed landing craft. He struck out on his own to develop the Ballbarrow, which won the Building Design Innovation Award in 1977, and five years and 5,127 prototypes later, perfected his Dual Cyclone™ no-loss-of-suction vacuum cleaner, now sold in more than 40 countries. Dyson founded a charity, the James Dyson Foundation, and in 2007 announced plans for the Dyson School of Design Innovation. Due to unforeseen zoning issues, the schedule of this initiative is currently pending. However, Dyson remains convinced, as he argues in this interview about his ambitions for the school, that hands-on science and technology education will reengage young people and reenergize economies.

You've been critical about the state of science and technology education—in the United Kingdom, at any rate. Why? Fewer and fewer people are studying engineering, physics, and technology. The reason I think this is important is that our wealth is determined by our ability to create technology and export it to the world. Now, you may make your products in China, you may assemble them in Malaysia, but as long as they're developed by, and the technology is owned by, American companies, Canadian companies, British companies, Japanese companies, it is an export from that country and it generates wealth for that country. So that's the underlying fiscal point. Because you might say, no one's interested in engineering, so give up on it. Well, why is it going wrong? From Dickensian times, never mind the last 50 years, the aristocracy and the educated class, even the working class, have steered people away from making things. And then the dot-com boom came along and that become

the ideal: you don't have to make anything, you just have to be clever. And education generally preaches that if you get good exams, you go to university; you don't have to get involved in factories and all that nasty, dirty work. And the media, which has become so powerful over the last 50 years, hasn't portrayed engineering as an exciting thing to do. My solution is to make engineering interesting and exciting.

The charitable organization you founded—the James Dyson Foundation—supports a number of educational initiatives, through awards, bursaries, and workshops. Exactly. We've gotten out into the classrooms. We see that children, from the ages of nine and 10 and, more crucially, 12 and 14 and 15, are fascinated by science. They love it, they're creative, they're inquisitive. They want to make models; they want to prove things out. Through our workshops, we've done surveys and we've found that two-thirds of these children want

71.

Consult with kids

Survey students about what they would like to study, then design spaces that let them learn what they want to learn.

BM: This is actually a pretty radical idea: to open source school, to say, "well, maybe the best source of information on this practice is the participants themselves." We assume they don't know anything, and I think that's the biggest mistake we make.

ER: With one project I worked on, we created design concepts, and then we interviewed 150 children—we asked them to critique and analyze the concepts, and they got to debate and then vote. These kids— and most of them are underprivileged—are really savvy. They know design; they understand color, and form; they understand plans and spatial relationships. And they have opinions. They have a huge aesthetic ability to select things. These kids basically created their learning environment and the way they used it.

—*Bruce Mau, Elva Rubio, BMD*

to take engineering as a major subject, but they can't. It doesn't exist. There is a desire there, so we're building what I hope will be the first of many engineering schools. It teaches 14- to 18-year-olds, and also teaches the first year of an undergraduate course.

Children should be marked on how many mistakes they make. Someone who gets it right the first time isn't learning anything.

Why a school? You could have done a curriculum; you could have done a virtual program. Because it's a very deep problem, and you've got to solve it culturally, starting right within a community. The school is in the city center, where cultural activities take place in the evenings. It's in Bath, but it could be anywhere, as long as it's in the city center. It has a cinema, a small one, which will show any film with any sort of engineering content. Could be about Henry Ford. Or even a science fiction film, a film about the future. We've got a cafe, and we've also got a…museum is the wrong word here. We've got a huge display area in the atrium, where we're working with the Science Museum, Williams F1, Rolls-Royce, Airbus. Engineering companies are very concerned about the same problems, so they'll come and talk to the kids about that broken Airbus wing, about why it snapped. We'll have an ever-changing exhibition of glamorous engineering and scientific objects.

What you've described sounds like a cultural center. Yes. That's the point. We want to inspire children to seek out engineering as a career, but we also want to change attitudes of parents and teachers to at last understand what technology and engineering are about, what physics is about. So it's no use this school being on the edge of town; it's got to be where we can pull people in, where they can walk in and have coffee and see what's on.

Can you talk more about some of the features of the school—the more formal learning spaces? It has a lot of workshops. It's very important to have an idea and quickly build what you need and test it and see if it works. And if it doesn't work, then try

and make it work. And during the process of making it work, you suddenly say, actually, what I need to understand here is hydrodynamics. So it forces you back into physics, and textbooks. It's key that they understand the theory, because we're linked to three fairly good engineering universities; we want to feed children into them, and they demand high academic achievement. Some engineers and scientists are high academic achievers; a lot are not. They get to being clever by understanding practical things, which inspires them to understand theory. What's happening in schools where they do teach design and technology is that, because workshops are expensive, it's becoming an entirely academic subject, where people write down their ideas to pass their exams. They don't make their idea then work out how to solve the problem, and the purpose of engineering and design is overcoming failure.

Failure is something schools generally want to stay far away from. That's another thing. I think it's very important for children to have failure, and lots of it. Because it shows that they're experimenting and understanding what works and what doesn't work. I've always said, children should be marked by how many mistakes they make. Someone who gets it right the first time isn't learning anything.

Some say that technology is pushing education toward virtual or at least on-line learning experiences. You seem to be arguing for going in the other direction, for grounding in the real world. I think there are ways you can do both. Two-thirds of children want to do engineering: The first thing is to locally satisfy that desire. And if you can then do it internationally, or even nationally, it's a very good idea. One of the things we want to develop is tools that can enable that. So if we find an interesting way of teaching something, or if we make a simple technical-drawing software, if we can then publish it on the web, an exciting curriculum can be created on a global basis. International cooperations and knowledge bases could be a very interesting part of future schools.

72.

Put theory into practice

Give students space— studios, workshops, and laboratories—where they can test ideas for practical applications.

The space doesn't have to be high-tech—and it doesn't even have to be inside the school. I saw some images of a student-designed billboard. This was a project where the kids were asked, "What's the one thing that you are proud of about your school and that you want to tell the world about?" The kids decided, and then they all designed the billboard. The project didn't just show the community the kids' creativity, it also galvanized the kids' sense of self-worth, and created a greater connection between the school and the community.

—Trung Le, OWP/P

The Illinois Math and Science Academy has a corporate-sponsored project called the Grainger Center. It makes lab space available for independent student work. The students propose a project, develop an experiment, and carry out the work, all in a completely flexible space.

—Rick Dewar, OWP/P

SPACE: THE CLASSROOM OF THE FUTURE

A TEACHER PRAISES AMERICA'S SPACE PROGRAM AND SPACE EXPLORERS FOR THEIR POWER TO INSPIRE LEARNING

Space is the ultimate classroom—a teacher-student paradise for discovery and learning. Schoolteacher Barbara Morgan experienced this firsthand while spending time, in 2007, aboard Space Shuttle Endeavour and the International Space Station as NASA's "Educator Astronaut." In addition to her "classroom" duties, holding educational events with schools on Earth via video link, Morgan helped deploy a truss segment to support electrical power systems required to operate the space station's science research laboratories.

For those who teach, Morgan's accomplishment is an inspiration. She carries with her the aspirations of every teacher to open minds to the thrill of learning and discovery, and America's commitment to space exploration can encourage a new generation of engineers and scientists. In the 1960s, the Apollo program gave a huge boost to technical education and career opportunities, and changed our world dramatically in the process. America's current space program—to complete assembly of the space station and develop the systems needed to support a return to the moon and future human missions to Mars—will open a new era of innovation and discovery.

While most teachers don't build spaceflight hardware or participate in breathtaking space walks, their labors in the classroom work hand-in-glove with NASA and its mission. Students want education with relevance and practical meaning. They want to make the world a better place. Their imaginations know no bounds. Unfortunately, their interest in and mastery of math, science, and engineering have waned. America's space program by itself can't fix this challenge, but it can help. The challenge of space travel excites students, and gives meaning to the hard work of science and math studies. Space exploration involves programs with real-world technical challenges that students and professionals can sink their teeth into. It creates high-tech jobs and career opportunities. It points a direction for the future, motivating our youth and all humanity to dream big and literally reach for the stars. Barbara Morgan—and all who teach—are opening another door for learning. **Adapted from:** "Space: a classroom for the future?"

For more: www.spacecoalition.com

73.
Expand virtually

Make sure a classroom has the capacity to link into learning opportunities beyond its four walls — even beyond the Earth itself.

We're getting to the point in the world where, at any level, you can contribute back to this global intellectual network. You don't have to be an academic to go on Wikipedia and edit an article. With the correct information and insight, anybody can do it. The whole world can do it. We're no longer discriminating in terms of how old you are or how young you are. That's really shifting the whole idea of research, and learning, and teaching.

—*Bruce Mau, BMD*

ERMA ORA BYRD CENTER FOR EDUCATIONAL TECHNOLOGIES
WHEELING, UNITED STATES

NASA MAKES ITS CUTTING-EDGE TECHNOLOGY AND
TRAINING TECHNIQUES AVAILABLE TO YOUNG PEOPLE

The Erma Ora Byrd Center for Educational Technologies houses cutting-edge educational technology in its 48,000-square foot facility. In addition to the Classroom of the Future, NASA's principal research and development center for educational technologies, the center houses the Challenger Learning Center, one of 51 worldwide, established by the Challenger Center for Space Science in memory of the space shuttle Challenger. The Learning Centers offer students the next best thing to actual space flight, with a Mission Control room designed after NASA Johnson Space Center and an orbiting space station. When students arrive at a Challenger Learning Center, they are first greeted by Learning Center representatives decked out in NASA flight suits. These flight directors, many of them former classroom teachers, provide an orientation briefing in which the students are given an overview of the mission, as well as their crew assignments. Many of the programs are built on simulation methods inspired by the way NASA trains America's astronauts. Educational simulations are dynamic models of real-world activity designed to allow students to face authentic conditions and problem solve just as their professional counterparts must.

Adapted from: "Challenger Center: Mission Simulations"

For more: www.challenger.org

TONYPANDY COMPREHENSIVE SCHOOL
PENYGRAIG, UNITED KINGDOM

A U.K. SCHOOL INSTALLS A REAL AND REVOLUTIONARY
MANUFACTURING TOOL AND ALLOWS STUDENTS TO
MAKE REAL THINGS

Tonypandy Comprehensive was the first school in the United Kingdom to install a CO_2 laser cutter, a revolutionary tool used in the world's most advanced factories. The laser represented a substantial investment by the school in developing its award-winning design technology department as a facility for prototypical computer-aided manufacturing. All students in years 7–13 produce three-dimensional design products using rapid prototyping methods. The laser can cut all manner of modern materials, with the exception of metals, with precision, leaving an edge that requires no further machining or finishing. Three-dimensional objects can be produced by the assembly of laser-cut layers to a design produced by pupils using a standard computer program such as Corel Draw. Because of the industrial specifications of the laser cutter, developed by technology company GCC, the students' work displays the most accurate of tolerances. **Adapted from:** "Laser cutter is school's launch pad to future" *Western Mail*

74.

Embrace purpose

Install technology that can simulate real-world situations—given the chance to solve authentic problems, kids will rise to the challenge.

LAKE GENEVA MIDDLE SCHOOL
LAKE GENEVA, UNITED STATES

A TEACHER AND STUDENTS DISCOVER THAT THE NEW OPEN CLASSROOM MAKES A NEW KIND OF LEARNING POSSIBLE

THE SCHOOL OF THE FUTURE
PHILADELPHIA, UNITED STATES

A SCHOOL DISTRICT PARTNERS WITH INDUSTRY TO TEST AN AFFORDABLE PAPERLESS CAMPUS

One of the biggest roadblocks to achieving integration of the physical and the virtual in K-12 classrooms is a set of time-honored presumptions of what a classroom should look like—such as, it should be rectangular, and have a front and a back. Grant Strobel has learned firsthand how different classroom architecture can change an instructor's teaching style.

Strobel is the tech ed teacher at Lake Geneva Middle School in Wisconsin. He works in the school's 2,600-square-foot Technology Center, an open classroom—no dividers, no cubicles—designed for a modular education program covering 18 different areas of technology. Built in 1999, the classroom is furnished with free-standing islands equipped with computers and a range of tools for hands-on projects and group problem solving. Each learning module covers a different technology, from radios to rockets, lasers to IT. Students work at the islands in pairs, but the classroom also has three work tables where they can gather in greater numbers.

Strobel says the design has changed his ideas about what constitutes effective teaching. "I'll never go back into a traditional classroom. The kids are so much more engaged in here. For one thing, it's completely hands-on. I'm not going to stand up in front of the classroom today and tell you how robots are used in the world or how rockets work. It's a completely different style of teaching." **Adapted from:** "A Movable Feast" **For more:** www.thejournal.com

The past decade has shown the impact of technology on education, and one can only imagine the advancements that the next 10 years will bring. One trend education experts are seeing is a move toward a paperless campus. The School District of Philadelphia and Microsoft Corporation partnered to explore this and other possibilities for the future of education. In September 2006, they opened the School of the Future in Philadelphia. Although Microsoft provided human capital, strategic planning tools and organizational best practices, it did not donate equipment, software or money to build the $63 million school. The project was completed on a traditional budget with the hope that it could become a replicable model for other schools.

The School of the Future is an almost paperless environment. An Interactive Learning Center replaces a traditional library. Students carry laptops instead of textbooks. Students have access to streaming media content on a variety of subjects from a variety of content experts. Administrators deliver announcements through live video broadcasts that each student can watch on his or her laptop.

In the classroom, a "virtual teaching assistant" provides teachers with online tracking to target student progress. Teachers can give assessments via computer during class. The software gauges the progress of each student and allows deeper instruction or review. **Adapted from:** "Design Trends"

For more: www.asumag.com

75.

Plan for the unknown

New technology brings with it new teaching opportunities – design a learning environment that will allow teachers to modify their methods and expectations as technology changes.

In 10 years, we're going to have a radically different understanding of education and school. That means anything fixed has to be built with transformational possibility. I don't know what that looks like. But it's really challenging as an idea. We're building schools without any acknowledgment of the transformation that is already underway, with the doubling of technological capacity every 12 months. So, figuring out how to build a platform for change, rather than a solution to the current circumstance, is quite a different design problem. The foundation has to be "We don't know" because as long as you're building it with the assumption that "Okay, ultimately we're going to figure this out and know what to do," you're closing down all kinds of possibilities.

—*Bruce Mau, BMD*

FROM BLACKBOARD TO WHITE-BOARD, THE SKY'S THE LIMIT

TEACHERS REPORT ON THE POSSIBILITIES OF ELECTRONIC
WHITEBOARDS THAT CONNECT WITH THE INTERNET, MARK
UP WITH A TOUCH, AND SAVE TO A COMPUTER FILE

"The whiteboard is good because you can get students who normally would not have come up to the blackboard to come up and add something to a diagram, for example, because they like using the board."

"Children are no longer afraid to be wrong. They realize that other students can add in their own thoughts and comments. So, one student can learn from the other."

"When I was teaching my class about pandas, I used the interactive whiteboard to connect to the Washington, DC, National Zoo's website and let my class watch the pandas on the Panda Cam.''

"I can use the annotation tools to put algebra formulas on the board or use the grid page feature to plot the growth and decay. Because all of the notes are saved within the software, I can go back and use the image file and easily review yesterday's lesson." **Adapted from:** "Interactive Whiteboards"
For more: www2.peterli.com/spm

76.

Unleash learning

Electronic learning aids aren't fancy window dressing: They offer teachers and students new and diverse ways to engage with subjects and ideas.

We hear all the time from educators who say, "We can't afford smartboards; we can't afford the technology." Well, I think we can't afford not to use technology. It's like investing in typewriters instead of keyboards. Both technologies can record words and thoughts but only one of them has the capacity for virtual connectivity.

—Helen Hirsh Spence, educational consultant to VS Furniture

DENVER SCHOOL OF SCIENCE AND TECHNOLOGY

DENVER, UNITED STATES

A STUDY OF A NEW TECHNOLOGY-FOCUSED SCHOOL REPORTS
RAPID SUCCESS IN OVERCOMING THE DIGITAL DIVIDE

The Denver School of Science and Technology (DSST) is dedicated to providing a diverse student body with an outstanding liberal arts high school education with a science and technology focus. To meet the school's goals, the instructional spaces are designed with mobile furniture and movable wall partitions for maximum flexibility.

DSST opened its doors with an ubiquitous computing environment. Hewlett Packard provided a grant that allowed DSST to become the first public high school in Colorado in which every student is provided with a wireless, networked personal computer. Students in grades 9 and 10 each receive a laptop, while students in grades 11 and 12 each receive a tablet computer.

DSST's vision for using educational technology notes that "The role of a liberal arts education is to enable and facilitate the creation of leaders who value community, individuals, and the creation of a truly human society."

The great majority of students say that the laptops have a very (65 percent) or somewhat (29 percent) positive impact on how much they learn in school. The students also report that the laptops positively influence how well they work with other students, how interested they are in school, their grades, and other things.

Data show that there was a "digital divide" for students before they began attending DSST. Among those who identify themselves as Hispanic, fully 50 percent report that they rarely or never used computers before they attended DSST. The corresponding figure for African American students is 40 percent, and 25 percent for Caucasian students. These figures may not be surprising but they support the importance of a laptop program in a public, ethnically diverse school serving large numbers of underrepresented students as a way to overcome the digital divide. **Adapted from:** *A Study of the 1:1 Laptop Program at the Denver School of Science & Technology* **For more:** dsst.colorado.edu

77.

Bridge the digital divide

One tested way to get all students, regardless of their socioeconomic background, up to speed technologically is to give them laptops and a place to be unplugged yet connected.

This makes me think of a project involving the Soros Foundation: They were putting up a satellite and designing a new software system for Mongolian education. Because, of course, in Mongolia, where much of the population is still nomadic, the children don't necessarily have a place where they go to study—studying goes with them. The foundation was instituting this technology to facilitate curriculum development when you're on the move. It's an extreme but interesting example where the learning space is not an actual space but a virtual space created by infrastructure.

—Monica Bueno, BMD

INGENIUM SCHOOLS
LONDON, UNITED KINGDOM

In 2001, Richmond upon Thames Council assembled a team to work on a vision for the classroom of the future. We started getting groups of teachers in to experience the room while we were still pulling it all together. A common question when they entered was "Where are all the computers?" There's not one to be seen, anywhere. The only visible concession to newer classroom technology is a projector for the main, curved screen. There are computers, of course, dozens of them, and cameras, video equipment, surround sound. But if you need it, you go and get it. It's not a computer lab. We're not too sure yet what it is, but "learning lab" will do for now.

What looked to us like a radical and high-tech school eight or nine years ago is looking pretty low-tech now. We're not just going to design a school or a classroom once and then sit back. We've got to keep moving; we've got to keep schools agile; we've got to keep testing our assumptions about what works and what doesn't work. And we're going to do that by looking around the world. Every school everywhere in the world is in a unique context and a unique culture; the trick is to look around the world for the best ingredients and assemble those ingredients into a local recipe. It's going to be what works in our context and our culture. And we find that out by listening to our teachers, and to our children. We're looking to produce the smartest kid and the happiest kid—we wants kids who are happy being smart and are happy being smart for the rest of their lives. So we've got to keep doing this year-on-year, in five years' time, in ten years' time, in fifty years' time. We've got to keep revisiting our assumptions.

—Stephen Heppell, technology and education consultant

Ingenium is a completely new approach to class-room design reflecting the demands of 21st-century learning. Our main source of ideas and inspiration has been Professor Stephen Heppell, formerly of Ultralab. Stephen is particularly interested in the design of spaces for learning, both real and virtual. We have also benefited from the involvement and support of Apple, Hewlett Packard, Microsoft, Mimio, Orange, Sony, and Steljes. Core members of the design team were students from the three partner schools. They told us they didn't want a rectangular box with desks: they wanted to be able to arrange the space to suit themselves; to have the resources they needed to be available on demand; and above all they wanted to feel comfort-able, in every sense, in their classroom.

Educators have long recognized that people learn in different ways. Traditional classrooms have responded less well to the kinesthetic type of learner—that is, one who learns best when they can move around, with space to practice and model. Here, the balance is redressed: supporting different learning styles is central to the design of the Ingenium. "Anytime, anywhere learning" is a well-worn phrase these days, and we wanted that philosophy to apply inside the classroom as well as outside. So all our equipment that can operate on batteries does, and our networkable equipment all communicates wirelessly. Of course, there are power and network points around for when you really need them, but most of the time we're glad not to have the clutter, and the restrictions of being tied down to one part of the room.

The range of learning resources available is being constantly expanded and updated, but typically consists of a projector for the main whiteboard, digital cameras, laptops, classroom voting system, portable IWB with Bluetooth slate, satellite TV, and video production including color keying.

The learning space lends itself to cooperative, group-based activities, as well as to presentations and performances. Four color-coded zones com-prising table, chairs, and whiteboard are arranged around a central, panoramic whiteboard. Groups can interact and students can work in their own groups as appropriate. All the furniture can be stacked in a special area out of the way at the rear. Full AV and lighting facilities maximize the impact of students' learning, creating a lively, exciting buzz.

All teachers using the space discuss their require-ments with an experienced curriculum advisor, who is able to suggest ways in which the room can add value to the learning experience and offer another pair of hands if needed for the activity. Making the most of the Ingenium involves understanding the special opportunities it affords. **Adapted from:** *Ingenium: BETT 07 Edition* **For more:** www.ingenium.org.uk

78.

Dream big and be brave

The rate of technological advancement is increasing exponentially. When designing schools, don't let today's reality limit tomorrow's possibilities.

WHAT WE LEARNED AT:
THE LONDON DESIGN DINNER
LONDON, UNITED KINGDOM

THE PROFESSIONALS TELL US HOW TO BEGIN THE
PROCESS OF DESIGNING BETTER SCHOOLS

We need a glossary of terms. For example, we struggle with knowing what to call the big, corridor-free spaces we're designing for new schools. We don't call them "open," because people have negative experiences with "open spaces" in schools. So we talk about agile buildings, and buildings that can be easily reconfigured."
—Dr. Stephen Heppell

At the Berlin workshop, the students' suggestions focused almost exclusively on what they are lacking. Plain and simple things, but so easily neglected: They have a tremendous longing for peace, because it's too noisy in the city; they have a tremendous need for flowers and plants in the building because there's too little green outside; and there's a tremendous desire for a sense of community. Their ideas and thoughts are an immense treasure. —Dr. Thomas Müller

We've talked about reform for a long time in education. It's actually beginning to happen, and it's really accelerating. This is absolutely a good moment. —Gareth Long

As design professionals, we want to know the requirement—what's this room for? But kids see things just as they are. My son picked up a pretzel and called it a cloud, a zero, a lasso. Kids can make something out of anything. As a program requirement, we have to allow these spaces to be anything. —Peter Brown

I asked the kids at the Berlin workshop what insight they had gained. They said they finally understood the concept of design—that with the right tools we can all be designers.
—Helen Hirsh Spence

Linda Sarate and the Little Village mothers were motivated to create change. All they knew initially was that they needed a new school— not what that meant or how to go about it. They had the foresight or luck to speak with the right organizations, to begin to gain that vocabulary. —Trung Le

This book full of narratives, ambition, and examples will build a sense of urgency, and it will also build a taxonomy. Children looking around their schools can't articulate what's wrong, they haven't got a vocabulary, they don't know any other experience. If we can give them a language of alternatives, we'll have lit the fuse. The 79 great ideas are going to grow to a million great ideas. That is what will change the world.
—Dr. Stephen Heppell

79.

Add to this list

The ideas in this book are ingredients, to be combined in varying quantities as suits conditions and tastes. The list is by no means finite. Add to it, adapt ideas, grow new ones, and transform the world.

A great place to start is thethirdteacher.com — log on and join the online conversation about the ideas in this book for transforming learning by design.

—The Third Teacher book team

ADD TO THIS LIST:
NOTES AND IDEAS

RESOURCES

Books

Architecture of Schools: The New Learning Environments, *Mark Dudek*
Describes a particularly specialized field encompassing ever changing educational theories, the subtle spatial and psychological requirements of growing children, and practical issues that are unique to these types of buildings.

Green Schools: Attributes for Health and Learning, *Committee to Review and Assess the Health and Productivity Benefits of Green Schools, National Research Council*
Examines the potential of environmentally-conscious school design for improving education.

Inventing Kindergarten, *Norman Brosteman*
Illustrates the founding principles of the original kindergarten, a then-revolutionary educational program invented in the 1830s by German educator Friedrich Froebel.

Learning Spaces, *Diana G. Oblinger, ed.*
Focuses on how learner expectations influence learning spaces, the principles and activities that facilitate learning, and the role of technology from the perspective of those who create learning environments.

Montessori: Educational Material for Early Childhood and Schools, *Thomas Müller, Romana Schneider, eds.*
Explores the main aspects of Montessori's theory of education, focusing primarily on the learning materials that are so critical to carrying out her philosophy.

Montessori: Science Behind the Genius, *Angeline Stoll Lillard*
Presents the research behind eight insights that are foundations of Montessori education, describing how each of these insights is applied in the Montessori classroom.

Opening Up Education: The Collective Advancement of Education through Open Technology, Open Content, and Open Knowledge, *Toru Iiyoshi, M. S. Vijay Kumar, eds.*
Collects essays by leaders in open education describing successes, challenges, and opportunities they have found in a range of open education initiatives.

Out of Our Minds: Learning to be Creative, *Sir Ken Robinson*
Argues for radical changes in how we should think about our own intelligence and creativity—and in how we should educate our children and each other to meet the challenges of living and working in the 21st century.

A Pattern Language: Towns, Buildings, Construction, *Christopher Alexander*
Offers a practical language for building and planning based on traditional architecture and natural considerations that create 253 "patterns." Twenty-five years after its publication, it is still one of the best-selling books on architecture.

Schools for Cities: Urban Strategies, *Sharon Haar, ed.*
Contains essays and current projects to demonstrate ways in which schools can contribute to a vital civic life.

Schulhausbau. Der Stand der Dinge / Der Schweizer Beitrag im Internationalen Kontext / School Buildings. The State of Affairs: The Swiss Contribution in an International Context, *Hochbaudepartement der Stadt Zurich, ed.*
Examines the consequences of school reforms for school design.

Teach Like Your Hair's on Fire, *Rafe Esquith*
Inspires readers with an account of a gifted teacher who transforms his fifth grade class. The only school teacher ever to receive the president's National Medal of Arts.

Thinking for Understanding: A Practical Resource for Teaching and Learning and Curriculum Development, *Melvin Freestone and Designshare, ed.*
Provides teachers with specific tools and techniques that they can use to make thinking a conscious and strategic activity for students.

Third Space: When Learning Matters, *Richard J. Deasy, Lauren M. Stevenson*
Describes the profound changes in the lives of kids, teachers, and parents in 10 economically disadvantaged communities across the country that use the arts to create great schools.

Whatever It Takes: Geoffrey Canada's Quest to Change Harlem and America, *Paul Tough*
Profiles educational visionary Geoffrey Canada, whose Harlem Children's Zone—currently serving more than 7,000 children—represents an audacious effort to end poverty within underserved communities.

A Whole New Mind: Why Right-Brainers Will Rule the Future, *Daniel Pink*
Describes how certain skill sets can be harnessed effectively in the dawning "Conceptual Age."

Websites/Organizations

General education Information:

nces.ed.gov
The National Center for Education Statistics is the primary federal entity for collecting and analyzing data related to education.

www.good.is/?p=12456
GOOD Sheet No. 005: Reform School. This is one of Good Magazine's "fact sheets," focusing on education design.

greatschoolsbydesign.com
This site is a national initiative of the American Architectural Foundation to improve the quality of America's schools and the communities they serve by promoting collaboration, excellence, and innovation in school design.

www.cefpi.org
The Council of Educational Facility Planners International's mission is to improve places where children learn.

archrecord.construction.com/projects/bts/archives/K-12
This site highlights examples and case studies of excellent K-12 school design collected by *Architectural Record* magazine.

www.bcse.uk.net
The British Council for School Environments is a membership organization made up of schools, local authorities, construction companies, architects, and all those involved in designing excellent learning environments. It acts as a forum for exchange, dialogue and advocacy.

edfacilities.org
Created by the U.S. Department of Education, the National Clearinghouse for Educational Facilities (NCEF) provides information on planning, designing, funding, building, improving, and maintaining safe, healthy, high performance schools.

schoolstudio.engr.wisc.edu
The School Design Research Studio at the University of Wisconsin-Madison seeks to advance the knowledge of effective physical environments for learning by promoting collaborative design and cooperative research.

www.cabe.org.uk
The Commission for Architecture and the Built Environment is the government's advisor on architecture, urban design and public space, providing guidance to architects, planners, designers, developers and clients.

www.oecd.org/edu/facilities
The OECD Programme on Educational Building (PEB) promotes the exchange and analysis of policy, research and experience in all matters related to educational building.

designshare.com
This site is a facilitator of ideas and resources about best practices and innovation in schools from early childhood through the university level.

www.school-works.org
This British schools design initiative offers an evolving resource of case studies of progressive practices, touching on all aspects of school design, as well as listings of literature, seminars and conferences.

www.montag-stiftungen.com/kooperationsprojekte.html
This German foundation supports pedagogical architecture.

www.archiv-der-zukunft.de/
This is a German NGO of reform oriented educators.

Basic needs:

www.epa.gov/iaq/schooldesign
This is a glossary and resource for creating healthy schools.

www.greenguard.org
The Greenguard Certification Program is an industry-independent, third-party testing program for low-emitting products and materials. Contains an online list whose products have met indoor air quality standards.

www.healthyschoolscampaign.org
This site advocates for policies and practices that allow all students, teachers and staff to learn and work in a healthy school environment.

www.quietclassrooms.org
This is an alliance of non-profit organizations working to create better learning environments in schools by reducing noise.

Minds at Work:

nifplay.org
The National Institute for Play unlocks the human potential through play in all stages of life using science to discover all that play has to teach us about transforming our world.

aep-arts.org
The Arts Education Partnership is a national coalition of arts, education, business, philanthropic and government organizations that demonstrate and promote the essential role of the arts in the learning and development of every child and in the improvement of America's schools.

Bodies in Motion:

www.iea.cc/ergonomics4children
Ergonomics for Children and Educational Environments provides a forum for the international exchange of scientific and technical ergonomics information related to children and educational environments.

ergo.human.cornell.edu
The Cornell University Ergonomics Web presents information from the Department of Design and Environmental Analysis at Cornell University. Contains computer-use guidelines for children of America's schools.

Community Connections:

www.826national.org
This is a family of seven nonprofit organizations dedicated to helping students, ages 6–18, with expository and creative writing.

www.lisc.org
Committed to helping neighbors build communities, LISC's national child care program is developing a series of "how-to" guides to assist organizations that are planning to renovate, construct or improve their early childhood facilities, including outdoor playgrounds.

kaboom.org

Kaboom rallies communities to achieve better public policy, funding and public awareness for increased play opportunities nationwide; provides resources, and publications for communities that wish to plan a new playspace on their own.

Sustainable Schools:

www.annex36.com

Sponsored by the International Energy Agency, the objective of Annex 36 is to provide tools and guidelines for energy-efficient retrofitting for decision-makers and designers to improve the learning and teaching environment of educational buildings in countries around the world.

www.buildgreenschools.org

The website of the U.S. Green Building Council assists in the creation of environmentally conscious school buildings by providing facts on the benefits of green schools, project profiles, news, videos, and guidance publications.

www.chps.net

The Collaborative for High Performance Schools facilitates the design, construction and operation of high performance schools—environments that are not only energy and resource efficient, but also healthy, comfortable, well lit, and contain the amenities for a quality education.

Realm of the Senses:

www.kidsgardening.org

An initiative of the National Gardening Association, this site provides a wide range of K-12 plant-based educational materials and programs.

Learning for All:

www.beyondaccess.org

This site contains information that guides parents, advocates, communities, play environment designers and equipment manufacturers in their efforts to create inclusive play environments for all children.

udeducation.org

This site supports educators and students in their teaching and study of universal design by offering instructional materials, essays on universal design, and a bibliography and links.

cast.org

A nonprofit research and development organization, CAST works to expand learning opportunities for all individuals, especially those with disabilities, through Universal Design for Learning.

Rewired Learning:

www.edutopia.org

The George Lucas Educational Foundation's website and magazine spreads the word about ideal, interactive learning environments and enables others to adapt these successes locally. This site also contains an archive of continually updated best practices.

www.futurelab.org.uk

Futurelab transforms the way people learn through innovative technology and practice, and develops the resources and practices that support new approaches to learning for the 21st century.

digitallearning.macfound.org

The MacArthur Foundation launched this initiative to help determine how digital technologies are changing the way young people learn, play, socialize, and participate in civic life. The website shares emerging research, blogs, awards.

insight.eun.org

An observatory for Information and Communication Technology in school education, Insight is designed to support decision-makers in education at national, regional or local levels to develop effective strategies for e-learning.

Film/Video

e² design

www.pbs.org/e2/design.html
e² design is an ongoing PBS series about the pioneers and innovators in the field of sustainable architecture, and how their work is producing solutions to pressing environmental and social challenges.

Sowing the Seeds for a More Creative Society

mitworld.mit.edu/video/372
In a video of a lecture in which MIT Media Lab professor, Mitchel Resnick describes how computers and technology should not be used merely to impart information, but to engage kids to design, create and invent. His work explores how new technologies can help people (especially children) learn new things in new ways.

TED: Ideas Worth Spreading *www.ted.com*
See Ken Robinson
Sir Ken Robinson makes an entertaining and profoundly moving case for creating an education system that nurtures (rather than undermines) creativity.
See Ann Cooper
Ann Cooper talks about the coming revolution in the way kids eat at school – local, sustainable, seasonal and even educational food.
See David Eggers
Dave Eggers asks the TED community to personally, creatively engage with local public schools. With spellbinding eagerness, he talks about how his 826 Valencia tutoring center inspired the opening of others around the world.

SOURCES

ALL LINKS IN THIS BOOK
WERE ACCURATE AT THE TIME
OF WRITING. UNLESS OTHER-
WISE NOTED, ALL STATISTICS
AND FUNDS ARE U.S.

Introduction

(p. 2) **From top to bottom**
"Statistics and Facts About High
School Drop out Rates," The Silent
Epidemic, www.silentepidemic
.org/epidemic/statistics-facts.htm

National School Design Institute:
A Report of Findings, American
Architectural Foundation, 2006,
www.schooldesign.org/aaf/
documents/report.nsdi.pdf

"New Report Sets Direction for
School Design in 21st Century,"
American Institute of Architects,
2007, www.aia.org/nwsltr_cae
.cfm?pagename=cae_a_200610
_new_report

Digest of Education Statistics,
2007 (NCES 2008-022), National
Center for Education Statistics,
U.S. Department of Education,
2008, www.nces.ed.gov/
programs/digest/d07/ch_2.asp

(p. 4) **From top to bottom**
Karl Fisch, Did You Know,
www.youtube.com/
watch?v=K04o2ic4g-A

A Touch of Greatness, Independent Lens, Independent
Television Service, www.pbs
.org/independentlens/
touchofgreatness/lessons.html#

Dominic Savage, quoted in
"Schoolchildren too big to squeeze
into chairs," by Polly Curtis,
guardian.co.uk (November 4,
2008), www.guardian.co.uk/
education/2008/nov/04/
bigchildren-chairs

National School Design Institute:
A Report of Findings, American
Architectural Foundation, 2006,
www.schooldesign.org/aaf/
documents/report.nsdi.pdf

Cassandra Rowand, "How Old
Are America's Public Schools?",
Education Statistics Quarterly
1, no. 1 (April 20, 1999), www
.nces.ed.gov/programs/quarterly/
Vol_1/1_1/4-esq11-h.asp#head1

Sean McDougall, quoted in "The
School of the Future," by Kim
Thomas, Futurelab, 2006, www
.futurelab.org.uk/resources/
publications_reports_articles/
web_articles/web_Article424

On Purpose Associates, "Neuroscience," Funderstanding, www
.funderstanding.com/content/
neuroscience

Ronald Kotulak, Inside the Brain,
summarized in "Twelve Design
Principles Based on Brain-based
Learning Research," by Jeffery A.
Lackney, School Design Research
Studio, schoolstudio.engr.wisc
.edu/brainbased.html

(p. 6) **From top to bottom**
Action Kit for Municipal Leaders:
Improving Public Schools—Issue
#5, National League of Cities,
Institute for Youth, Education, and
Families, www.nlc.org/ASSETS/
DE754D45E9AC4A5198A306F2
F00E0023/Improving%20PS%20
Action%20Kit.pdf

Condition of Education, National
Center for Education Statistics,
U.S. Department of Education,
2001, in "Asthma Facts and
Figures," Asthma and Allergy Foundation of America, www.aafa.org/
display.cfm?id=8&sub=42#_ftn12

Dr. Dieter Breithecker, Enjoying
School, Fun in Learning, Federal
Working Group on the Development of Posture and Exercise,
www.bag-haltungundbewegung
.de/fileadmin/bag/binary/BAG2_
Enjoying_0302_E.pdf

Robert Balfanz and Nettie Legters,
Locating the Dropout Crisis.
Which High Schools Produce
the Nation's Dropouts? Where
Are They Located? Who Attends
Them?, Center for Research on
the Education of Students Placed
at Risk, John Hopkins University,
www.eric.ed.gov/ERICWebPortal/
contentdelivery/servlet/
ERICServlet?accno=ED484525

Dr. Dieter Breithecker, Enjoying
School, Fun in Learning, Federal
Working Group on the Development of Posture and Exercise,
www.bag-haltungundbewegung.
de/fileadmin/bag/binary/BAG2_
Enjoying_0302_E.pdf

Sir Ken Robinson, Sir Ken Robinson: Do schools kill creativity?,
TED, www.ted.com/index.php/
talks/ken_robinson_says_schools_
kill_creativity.html

(p. 8) **From top to bottom**
J. M. Lowe, "The interface between
educational facilities and learn-
ing climate in three elementary
schools," PhD. diss., Texas A&M
University, in Do School Facilities
Affect Academic Outcomes?, by
Mark Schneider, National Clearing-

house for Educational Facilities,
2002, www.edfacilities.org/pubs/
outcomes.pdf

Action Kit for Municipal Leaders:
Improving Public Schools—Issue
#5, National League of Cities,
Institute for Youth, Education, and
Families, www.nlc.org/ASSETS/
DE754D45E9AC4A5198A306F2
F00E0023/Improving%20PS%20
Action%20Kit.pdf

Digest of Education Statistics,
2007 (NCES 2008-022), National
Center for Education Statistics,
U.S. Department of Education,
2008, www.nces.ed.gov/
programs/digest/d07/ch_2.asp

Census at School, Statistics
Canada, www19.statcan.
ca/04/04_0708/04_0708_
020-eng.htm

Michael R. Bloomberg, "Flabby,
Inefficient, Outdated," Mike-
Bloomberg.com (December 14,
2006), www.mikebloomberg.com/
index.cfm?objectid=8F530AF0
-1D09-317F-BBA0E8C7BE4E89F9

(p. 10) **From top to bottom**
Mark Schneider, Do School Facilities Affect Academic Outcomes?,
National Clearinghouse for Educational Facilities, 2002, www.ed
facilities.org/pubs/outcomes.pdf

W.J. Hussar and T.M. Bailey, Projec-
tions of Education Statistics to
2016 (NCES 2008-060), National
Center for Education Statistics,
U.S. Department of Educa-
tion, 2007, www.nces.ed.gov/
pubs2008/2008060.pdf

Renate Nummela Caine and
Geoffrey Caine, Education at the
Edge of Possibility, Alexandria, VA:
Association for Supervision and
Curriculum Development, 1997.

"George Bernard Shaw,"
Wikiquote, en.wikiquote.org/w/
index.php?title=George_Bernard
_Shaw&oldid=857440

"John F. Kennedy," To Inspire,
www.toinspire.com/author.
asp?author=John+F.+Kennedy

Barack Obama, "Remarks of Senator Barack Obama: Our Kids, Our
Future," Obama for America, www
.barackobama.com/2007/11/20/
remarks_of_senator_barack_
obam_34.php

1 Basic Needs

(p. 26) **From top to bottom**
Attacking Asthma, Combating an
epidemic among our children:

A Report to the Senate Committee
on Post Audit and Oversight of
the Massachusetts Senate, The
Commonwealth of Massachusetts,
2002, and "Health, United States,
2005," Center for Disease Control,
in Greening America's Schools:
Costs and Benefits, by Gregory
Kats, Capital E, 2006, www
.cap-e.com/ewebeditpro/items/
059F9819.pdf

Gregory Kats, Greening America's
Schools: Costs and Benefits,
Capital E, 2006, www.cap-e.com/
ewebeditpro/items/059F9819.pdf

Carnegie Mellon University Center
for Building Performance, in
Greening America's Schools: Costs
and Benefits, by Gregory Kats,
Capital E, 2006, www.cap-e.com/
ewebeditpro/items/059F9819.pdf

Building Minds, Minding Buildings:
Turning Crumbling Schools into
Environments for Learning, American Federation of Teachers, 2006,
www.aft.org/topics/building
-conditions/downloads/minding
-bldgs.pdf

Gregory Kats, Greening America's
Schools: Costs and Benefits,
Capital E, 2006, www.cap-e.com/
ewebeditpro/items/059F9819.pdf

Mark Schneider, Do School Facilities Affect Academic Outcomes?,
National Clearinghouse for Educational Facilities, 2002, www
.edfacilities.org/pubs/outcomes.pdf

(p. 27) **From top to bottom**
"School Facilities: America's
Schools not Designed or
Equipped for the 21st Century,"
General Accounting Office Report #
HEHS-95-95, in Greening America's
Schools: Costs and Benefits, by
Gregory Kats, Capital E, 2006,
www.cap-e.com/ewebeditpro/
items/059F9819.pdf

"Indoor Air Quality," U.S. Environmental Protection Agency, 2003,
www.epa.gov/iaq/

Mark Schneider, Do School Facilities Affect Academic Outcomes?,
National Clearinghouse for Educational Facilities, 2002, www
.edfacilities.org/pubs/outcomes.pdf

Mark Waldecker, "American School
& University: Creating Positive,
High Performance Learning
Environments," KI Education,
www.kieducation.com/issues
.aspx?ar=86

"School Facilities: America's
Schools not Designed or Equipped
for the 21st Century," General

Accounting Office Report # HEHS-95-95, in *Greening America's Schools: Costs and Benefits*, by Gregory Kats, Capital E, 2006, www.cap-e.com/ewebeditpro/items/059F9819.pdf

(p. 34) Basic Needs Come First
"Maslow's Hierarchy of Basic Needs," Investing in Children, www.investinginchildren.on.ca/Communications/articles/maslow.html

(p. 36) Physiological Vulnerability of School Children
Sherry Everett Jones, Robert Axelrad and Wendy A. Wattigney, "Healthy and Safe School Environment, Part II, Physical School Environment: Results From the School Health Policies and Programs Study 2006," *Journal of School Health* 77, no. 8 (October 2007), www.ashaweb.org/files/public/JOSH_1007/josh77_8_jones_p544.pdf

(p. 38) Indoor Air Quality as a Learning Opportunity
Carolyn Marshall, *Indoor Air Quality in Canadian Schools: Final Report*, The Indoor Air Quality (IAQ) in Canadian Schools Project and Atlantic Health Promotion Research Center, Dalhousie University, 2003, www.ahprc.dal.ca/Final%20Report.pdf

(p. 38) Perspectives on Indoor Air Quality
"Actions to Improve Indoor Air Quality," U.S. Environmental Protection Agency, www.epa.gov/iaq/schools/actions_to_improve_iaq.html

(p. 40) Guardians of the Indoor Environment
Michael A. Berry, *Introduction to Take a Deep Breath and Thank Your Custodian*, Jennie Young, ed., National Education Association Health Information Network, 2004, www.neahin.org/programs/environmental/IAQ.custodian.guide.pdf

(p. 42) Strategies for Enhancing Wanted Sounds
Ewart A. Wetherill, "Classroom Design for Good Hearing," Quiet Classrooms, www.quietclassrooms.org/library/goodhearing.htm

(p. 44) Thomas Deacon Academy
"Thomas Deacon Academy opens for the new school year" (press release), Foster + Partners, 2007.

(p. 45) Thomas Deacon Academy
"About BSF: Better Secondary School Buildings to Support

Educational Reform," Teachernet, Department for Children, Schools, and Families, 2007, www.teachernet.gov.uk/management/resourcesfinanceandbuilding/bsf/aboutbsf/

(p. 46) Thomas Deacon Academy
Eleanor Baxter, interview with Angelica Fox, email, December 2008.

2 Minds at Work

(p. 52) From top to bottom
William Deresiewicz, "The Disadvantages of an Elite Education," *The American Scholar* (Summer 2008), www.theamericanscholar.org/su08/elite-deresiewicz.html

Sean McDougall, quoted in "The School of the Future," by Kim Thomas, Futurelab, 2006, www.futurelab.org.uk/resources/publications_reports_articles/web_articles/web_Article424

"Record Investment in Music, Arts & PE," Office of the Governor of the State of California, www.gov.ca.gov/index.php?/fact-sheet/3699/

Kimberly Seltzer and Tom Bentley, *The Creative Age: Knowledge and Skills for the New Economy*, London: Demos, 1999, www.demos.co.uk

Currently, Demos publications are licensed under a Creative Commons Attribution-NonCommercial-NoDerivs 2.0 England & Wales License.

Users are welcome to download, save, perform or distribute this work electronically or in any other format, including in foreign language translation without written permission subject to the conditions set out in the Creative Commons license.

The Imagine Nation Poll, The Imagine Nation and Lake Research Partners, www.theimaginenation.net/resources.htm

Marshall McLuhan and Quentin Fiore, *The Medium is the Massage*, Toronto: Penguin Canada, 2003.

(p. 53) From top to bottom
"Imagination," World of Quotes, www.worldofquotes.com/topic/Imagination/1/index.html

Richard Florida, *Who's Your City? How the Creative Economy is Making Where to Live the Most Important Decision of Your Life*, Toronto: Random House Canada, 2008.

"Creative quotes and quotations: On the Mind," *CreatingMinds*, www.creatingminds.org/quotes/mind.htm

Paul Pastorek, quoted in "A Teachable Moment," by Paul Tough, *The New York Times Magazine*, August 14, 2008, www.nytimes.com/2008/08/17/magazine/17NewOrleans-t.html?pagewanted=1&_=1&sq=education&st=cse&scp=2

Arts & Economic Prosperity III: The Economic Impact of Nonprofit Arts and Culture Organizations and Their Audiences, Americans for the Arts, www.americansforthearts.org/information_services/research/services/economic_impact/default.asp

"Carl Sagan," *Wisdom Quotes*, www.wisdomquotes.com/001502.html

(p. 60) Neurological Growth Spurts
Maria Fusaro, "What's the Brain Got to do with it?", summary of "Growth cycles of brain and mind," by K. W. Fischer and S. P. Rose, *Educational Leadership* 56, no. 3 (1998), www.uknow.gse.harvard.edu/learning/learning002a.html

(p. 60) Right Brain, New Mind
Robert Sylwester, "Cognitive Neuroscience Discoveries and Educational Practices," *The School Administrator* (December 2006), www.aasa.org/publications/saarticledetail.cfm?ItemNumber=7814

(p. 62) Moving as Thinking
Sir Ken Robinson, *Sir Ken Robinson: Do schools kill creativity?*, TED, www.ted.com/index.php/talks/ken_robinson_says_schools_kill_creativity.html

(p. 64) Howard Gardner Smart Spaces for all Learners
Howard Gardner, "Why Multiple Intelligences Theory Continues to Thrive," Danish University of Education, www.dpu.dk/site.aspx?p=8649&newsid1=4440

(p. 66) Learning in Museums
Shari Tishman, "Learning in Museums," *College Art Association News* 30, no. 5 (September 2005), www.collegeart.org/pdf/caa-news-09-05.pdf

(p. 66) Henry Ford Museum
Carolyn Jabs, "Creating Classrooms: It Takes a Village—and a Museum," *Edutopia, The George Lucas Educational Foundation*

(November 2004), www.edutopia.org/it-takes-village-and-museum

(p. 68) Key Learning Community
Beverly Hoeltke and Mary G. Staten, "Key Learning Community—Flow Theory," Indiana Public Schools, www.616.ips.k12.in.us/Theories/Flow/default.aspx

(p. 72) Ministry of Education New High Schools
Angela Martins, interview with Trung Le, tape recording, September 2008.

3 Bodies in Motion

(p. 78) From top to bottom
Morgan Clendaiel, "Fall Down Go Boom," *Good Magazine*, September/October 2008.

Centers for Disease Control and Prevention, 2006, in *Children and Nature 2008: A Report on the Movement to Reconnect Children to the Natural World*, by Cheryl Charles et al., Children & Nature Network, 2008, www.childrenandnature.org/uploads/CNMovement.pdf

University of Michigan Institute for Social Research, 1998, in "Children Study Longer and Play Less, a Report Says," by Steven A. Holmes, *The New York Times*, November 11, 1998, query.nytimes.com/gst/fullpage.html?res=950CE0DD1F3EF932A25752C1A96E958260&sec=&spon=&pagewanted=1

Mark Waldecker, "High Class," *American School & University* 78, no. 2 (October 2005), www.asumag.com/mag/university_high_class/

Wikiquote contributors, "Confucius," *Wikiquote*, en.wikiquote.org/w/index.php?title=Confucius&oldid=829583

This quotation has been attributed to various authors, including Lao Tzu and Confucian scholars.

Susan Herrington, "Outdoor Spaces," in *Schools and Kindergartens: A Design Manual*, by Mark Dudek et al., Berlin: Birkhauser Verlag AG, 2007.

(p. 79) From top to bottom
Fish, 1984, cited in Knight and Noyes, 1999, in "Get Techfit" Guidelines, by Diane Tien, Cornell University Ergonomics Web, www.ergo.human.cornell.edu/mbergo/schoolguide.html

Bös 1999, in *Ergonomics for children*, by Dr. D. Breithecker,

Federal Working Group on the Development of Posture and Exercise, www.bag-haltungundbewegung.de/fileadmin/bag/binary/ergonomics_children.pdf

Balague, 1988 and Davoine, 1991, both cited in Mandal, 1997, in "Get Techfit" Guidelines, by Diane Tien, Cornell University Ergonomics Web, www.ergo.human.cornell.edu/mbergo/schoolguide.html

Stuart Brown, "The Importance of Play," *The New York Times Magazine,* February 17, 2008.

Dr. D. Breithecker, *Ergonomics for children,* Federal Working Group on the Development of Posture and Exercise, www.bag-haltungundbewegung.de/fileadmin/bag/binary/ergonomics_children.pdf

Morgan Clendaiel, "Fall Down Go Boom," *Good Magazine,* September/October 2008.

(p. 86) **Perspectives Charter School**
Case Study: Perspectives Charter School, Chicago, Illinois, VS America, Inc.

(p. 88) **Engaged Learning**
James McDonough, "Engaged Learning," *American School & University* (May 1, 2000) © 2000 Penton Media. All rights reserved. www.asumag.com/mag/university_engaged_learning/

(p. 90) **Invitation to Play**
Schools for the Future: Inspirational Design for PE & Sports Spaces, Department for Education and Skills, 2005, publications. teachernet.gov.uk/default.aspx?PageFunction=productdetails&PageMode=publications&ProductId=DFES-2064-2005&

(p. 92) **Hampden Gurney Church of England Primary School**
Organization for Economic Cooperation and Development, PEB *Compendium of Exemplary Educational Facilities,* 3rd edition, France: OECD Publishing, 2006.

(p. 94) **Brains in Motion**
Renate Nummela Caine et al., *12 Brain/Mind Learning Principles in Action: The Fieldbook for Making Connections, Teaching, and the Human Brain,* Thousand Oaks, CA: Corwin Press, 2005.

(p. 94) **Playgrounds and the War Against Obesity**
Stacy St. Clair, "Pump Up the Fun: What's new on the playground?,"

Recreation Management 8, no. 7 (July 2007), www.recmanagement.com/200707fe02.php

(p. 96) **Creating Playgrounds Kids Love**
Vicki L. Stoecklin, "Creating Playgrounds Kids Love," White Hutchinson Leisure & Learning Group, www.whitehutchinson.com/children/articles/playgrndkidslove.shtml

(p. 96) **Kids Talk About Playing**
Catherine Burke, "Play in Focus: Children Researching Their Own Spaces and Places for Play," *Children, Youth and Environments* 15, no. 1 (2005), www.colorado.edu/journals/cye/15_1/a2_PlayInFocus.pdf

(p. 100) **Fridtjof Nansen School**
Vivian Barnekow et al., Health-promoting schools: a resource for developing indicators, International Planning Committee (IPC) of the European Network of Health Promoting Schools, 2006, www.schoolsforhealth.eu/upload/pubs/Healthpromotingschoolsaresourcefordevelopingindicators.pdf

Dr. D. Breithecker, The Educational Workplace, Federal Working Group on the Development of Posture and Exercise, www.bag-haltungundbewegung.de/fileadmin/bag/binary/BAG-Endbericht-k_US.pdf

Dr. D. Breithecker, Physically Active Schoolchildren – alert heads, Federal Working Group on the Development of Posture and Exercise, www.bag-haltungundbewegung.de/fileadmin/bag/binary/BAG4_USLetter.pdf

Dr. D. Breithecker and Hermann Stadtler, "Mut tut gut! Das wichtige Spiel der kinder mit ihren Grenzen," Fridtjof Nansen Schule, www.fns-online.de/download/index.html

4 Community Connections

(p. 106) **From top to bottom**
George Lucas, "A Word from George Lucas: Edutopia's Role in Education," *Edutopia, The George Lucas Educational Foundation,* www.edutopia.org/lucas

"K-12 School Improvement: Why Municipal Leaders Make Education a City Priority," National League of Cities, Institute for Youth, Education, and Families, www.nlc.org/IYEF/education/K-12_school/index.aspx

Tracey Burns, "Learning and teaching, schools and communities," *Journal of Educational Change* 9 (2008), www.springerlink.com/content/rh15l316227u3512/

Malcolm Gladwell, *The Tipping Point: How Little Things Can Make a Big Difference,* Boston: Back Bay Books, 2002.

Adriana de Kanter et al., *21st Century Community Learning Centers: Providing Quality After-school Learning Opportunities for America's Families,* U.S. Department of Education, 2000, www.eric.ed.gov/ERICWebPortal/contentdelivery/servlet/ERICServlet?accno=ED445795

Action Kit for Municipal Leaders: Improving Public Schools—Issue #5, National League of Cities, Institute for Youth, Education, and Families, www.nlc.org/ASSETS/DE754D45E9AC4A5198A306F2F00E0023/Improving%20PS%20Action%20Kit.pdf

(p. 107) **From top to bottom**
Kathryn Riley, "Can schools successfully meet their educational aims without the clear support of their local communities?", *Journal of Educational Change* 9 (2008), www.springerlink.com/content/5l12059347859137/

Americans' Attitudes Toward Walking and Creating Better Walking Communities, Belden Russonello & Stewart Research and Communications, 2003, www.brspoll.com/Reports/walkingrelease.pdf

Wikipedia contributors, "It Takes a Village," *Wikipedia, The Free Encyclopedia,* www.en.wikipedia.org/w/index.php?title=It_Takes_a_Village&oldid=252516753

Superintendent Dr. Reginald Mayo, quoted in *Stronger Schools, Stronger Cities: A Report on the Municipal Leadership in Education Project,* by Audrey M. Hutchinson and Denise Van Wyngaardt, National League of Cities, Institute for Youth, Education, and Families, 2004, www.nlc.org/ASSETS/E28C6B537E7C4D7D84B74CB2D95175C8/IYEF_Stronger_Cities.pdf

Centers for Disease Control and Prevention, 2006, in *Children and Nature 2008: A Report on the Movement to Reconnect Children to the Natural World,* by Cheryl Charles et al., Children & Nature Network, 2008, www

.childrenandnature.org/uploads/CNMovement.pdf

"American Education Week, November 11–17, 2007 Education Quotes," National Education Association, www.nea.org/aew/quotes.html

(p. 114) **A Short History of American Public Education**
Sharon Haar, ed., *Schools for Cities: Urban Strategies,* National Endowment for the Arts, New York: Princeton Architectural Press, 2002.

(p. 116) **New Columbia Community Campus**
Chelsea Houy, "Textbook Tech," *Archi-Tech Mag* (April 2007), www.architechmag.com/articles/detail.aspx?contentID=3676

"American Architectural Foundation And Knowledgeworks Foundation Announce Winner of 2007 Richard Riley Award," American Architectural Foundation, www.archfoundation.org/aaf/aaf/News.45.htm

(p. 118) **Evangelische Comprehensive School**
Peter Hübner, *Evangelische Gesamtschule Gelsenkirchen-Bismarck: Kinder Bauen Iher Schule / Children Make Their Own School,* Bilingual edition, Fellbach, Germany: Edition Axel Menges, 2006.

(p. 120) **Schoolyards as Tools for Neighborhood Revitalization**
Thomas M. Menino, "Designing Schoolyards & Building Community," The Boston Schoolyard Initiative, www.schoolyards.org/text/Schoolyard.pdf

(p. 122) **Building a School, Reconstructing a Community**
Carolyn Edwards, George Forman and Lalla Gandini, *The Hundred Languages of Children: The Reggio Emilia Approach Advanced Reflections,* 2nd Edition, New York: Ablex Publishing, 1998.

(p. 124) **Rosa Parks Elementary School**
Mahlum Architects, "Rosa Parks Elementary School Students Walk, Bicycle Rather Than Take the Bus," *Environmental Design + Construction* (July 11, 2007), www.edcmag.com/CDA/Archives/BNP_GUID_9-5-06_A_10000000000000133925

(p. 130) **Chicago Public Schools**
Richard Daley, "Delivering Sustainable Communities

Summit Address," Speech, Manchester, U.K., February 2005, egov.cityofchicago.org

5 Sustainable Schools

(p. 136) **From top to bottom**
Gregory Kats, *Greening America's Schools: Costs and Benefits,* Capital E, 2006, www.cap-e.com/ewebeditpro/items/059F9819.pdf

Gregory Kats, *Greening America's Schools: Costs and Benefits,* Capital E, 2006, www.cap-e.com/ewebeditpro/items/059F9819.pdf

Hashem Akbari Lawrence Berkeley National Laboratory, in *Greening America's Schools: Costs and Benefits,* by Gregory Kats, Capital E, 2006, www.cap-e.com/ewebeditpro/items/059F9819.pdf

"Benefits of Green Schools," U.S. Green Building Council, www.buildgreenschools.org/press/benefits.html

Al Gore, quoted in "Stars join Clinton's campaign to save the world," *ABC News,* September 27, 2007, www.abc.net.au/news/stories/2007/09/27/2045263.htm

"Benefits of Green Schools," U.S. Green Building Council, www.buildgreenschools.org/press/benefits.html

(p. 137) **From top to bottom**
Timothy Smith et al., *Effects of Energy Needs and Expenditures on U.S. Public Schools* (NCES 2003-018), National Center for Education Statistics, U.S. Department of Education, 2003, www.nces.ed.gov/pubs2003/2003018.pdf

J. Brown, P. Plympton and K. Stevens, *High-Performance Schools: Affordable Green Design for K-12 Schools* (NREL/CP-710-34967), 2004 ACEEE Summer Study on Energy Efficiency in Buildings, 2004.

"Benefits of Green Schools," U.S. Green Building Council, www.buildgreenschools.org/press/benefits.html

Timothy Smith et al., *Effects of Energy Needs and Expenditures on U.S. Public Schools* (NCES 2003-018), National Center for Education Statistics, U.S. Department of Education, 2003, www.nces.ed.gov/pubs2003/2003018.pdf

David Orr, "What Is Education For?

Six myths about the foundations of modern education and six new principles to replace them," *In Context,* no. 27 (Winter 1991), www.context.org/ICLIB/IC27/Orr.htm

(p. 144) **Elements of a Sustainable School**
"CHPS Overview No. 4. What is a High Performance High School?", The Collaborative for High Performance Schools, Inc., www.chps.net/chps_schools/overviewWhatIs.htm

(p. 146) **Kvernhuset Junior High School**
Karin Buvik, "Bringing the outside inside," *Children in Europe,* March 2005.

(p. 148) **Students Praise Green**
Generation G Film, Kontentreal Productions, www.kontentreal.com

(p. 152) **The Savings of Green**
J. Brown, P. Plympton and K. Stevens, *High-Performance Schools: Affordable Green Design for K-12 Schools* (NREL/CP-710-34967), 2004 ACEEE Summer Study on Energy Efficiency in Buildings, 2004.

(p. 154) **Charlottesville Waldorf School**
"Commitment to the Power of Two," *The Acorn 3,* no. 2 (Fall 2007), www.greenestschool.org/images/stories/acorn_fall_2007.pdf

(p. 157) **IslandWood School**
Richard Louv, *Last Child in the Woods,* revised and updated version, New York: Algonquin Books of Chapel Hill, 2008.

(p. 158) **IslandWood School**
"IslandWood: A School in the Woods," DesignShare, www.designshare.com/index.php/projects/islandwood/narratives

Debbi Brainerd, "History of Island Wood," and Pat Guild O'Rourke, "What is Island Wood," New Horizons for Learning, www.newhorizons.org/strategies/environmental/front_environmental.htm

6 Realm of the Senses

(p. 164) **From top to bottom**
Jamie Oliver, *Killer Facts About Our Weight Problem,* Feed Me Better, 2006, www.jamieoliver.com/media/jo_sd_killer_facts.pdf?phpMyAdmin=06af156b76166043e2845ee292db12ee

Juhani Pallasmaa, "Embodied Experience and Sensory Thought," *Educational Philosophy and*

Theory 39, no. 7 (December 2007).

"Come to Your Senses: Your Sense of Touch," Oracle Education Foundation, ThinkQuest, library.thinkquest.org/3750/touch/touch.html

Christopher Alexander et al., *A Pattern Language,* New York: Oxford University Press, 1977.

Gavin Ambrose and Paul Harris, *Colour: Basics Design,* Chicago: AVA Publishing, 2005.

(p. 165) **From top to bottom**
"What Are Taste Buds?", KidsHealth, www.kidshealth.org/kid/talk/qa/taste_buds.html

Johann Pestalozzi, quoted in *Inventing Kindergarten,* by Norman Brosterman, New York: H.N. Abrams, 1997.

Qais Faryadi, "The Montessori Paradigm of Learning: So What?" Ph.D. diss., UiTM Malaysia, 2007.

"George Sheehan," *ThinkExist,* thinkexist.com/quotes/george_sheehan/

Jeff Goldberg, "Quivering: Bundles That Let Us Hear," in *Seeing, Hearing, and Smelling the World: New Findings Help Scientists Make Sense of Our Senses,* The Howard Hughes Medical Institute, 1995, www.hhmi.org/senses/

(p. 172) **The Edible Schoolyard**
Carey Jones, "An Interview with Alice Waters," *Montessori Life* (April 1, 2005), www.findarticles.com/p/articles/mi_qa4097/is_200504/ai_n14686845

(p. 172) **School Food Hero**
Niko Griffin, "Local volunteer transforms pupil's attitudes to vegetables in a successful school gardening club," School Food Trust, www.schoolfoodtrust.org.uk/casestudy-detail.asp?caseid=39

(p. 174) **The Tactile Body**
Eric Haseltine, "How Your Brain Sees You," *Discover* (September 2005), www.findarticles.com/p/articles/mi_m1511/is_/ai_64698214

(p. 178) **Creating a Workshop for the Senses**
Matti Bergstrom and Pia Ikonen, "Space to play, room to grow," *Children in Europe,* March 2005.

(p. 180) **What Color for What Room**
Ellen Kollie, "Light and Color Goes to School," *College Planning*

& Management 7, no. 6, (June 2004), www2.peterli.com/spm/resources/articles/archive.php?article_id=842

(p. 182) **The Child's Expanding World**
David Sobel, "Beyond Ecophobia," *Orion Magazine,* Autumn 1995.

(p. 185) **Hellerup School**
Ulla Kjærvang, "Power of Aesthetics to Improve Student Learning," DesignShare, www.designshare.com/index.php/articles/aesthetics-and-learning/

(p. 186) **Hellerup School**
Anne Strange Stelzner, *Without shoes, without inhibitions—ready for learning—School Hellerup, Denmark,* Arkitema Architects.

7 Learning for All

(p. 192) **From top to bottom**
NEA Report on the Individual's with Disabilities Education Act, 1997, National Education Association, in *Creating Accessible Schools,* by James Ansley, National Clearinghouse for Educational Facilities, 2000, www.edfacilities.org/pubs/accessibility.pdf

The Digest of Educational Statistics, 2001, U.S. Department of Education, in *Accessible Technology: A Guide for Educators,* Microsoft in Education, download.microsoft.com/download/7/d/b/7db02f2c-2446-44a3-b22d-66f530f254a2/Accessible_Technology.doc

"About Us," National Center for Boundless Playgrounds, www.boundlessplaygrounds.org/about/faq.php#top

Findings From The Condition of Education 2008: Enrollment, Student Diversity on the Rise, National Center for Education Statistics, nces.ed.gov/programs/coe/press/COE_2008_Highlights.pdf

Edward Steinfeld, *Education for All: The Cost of Accessibility,* The World Bank, 2005, siteresources.worldbank.org/DISABILITY/Resources/280658-1172610312075/EFACostAccessibility.pdf

National Assessment of Educational Progress, 2005, in "Our nation's greatest injustice," Teach For America, www.teachforamerica.org/mission/greatest_injustice.htm

Susan Peters, *Education for All: Including Children with Disabilities,* The World Bank, 2003, siteresources.worldbank.org/ DISABILITY/Resources/280658 -1172610312075/EFAIncluding .pdf

(p. 193) **From top to bottom**
James Ansley, *Creating Accessible Schools,* National Clearinghouse for Educational Facilities, 2000, www.edfacilities.org/pubs/ accessibility.pdf

National Center for Children in Poverty, 2006, in "Our nation's greatest injustice," Teach For America, www.teachforamerica.org/ mission/greatest_injustice.htm

Accessible Technology: A Guide for Educators, Microsoft in Education, download.microsoft.com/ download/7/d/b/7db02f2c-2446 -44a3-b22d-66f530f254a2/ Accessible_Technology.doc

Barack Obama, "Remarks of Senator Barack Obama: Our Kids, Our Future," Obama for America, www .barackobama.com/2007/11/20/ remarks_of_senator_barack _obam_34.php

Mark Twain and Brian Collins, ed., *When in Doubt, Tell the Truth: And Other Quotations from Mark Twain,* New York: Columbia University Press, 1996.

National Assessment of Educational Progress, 2005, in "Our nation's greatest injustice," Teach For America, www.teachforamerica .org/mission/greatest_injustice.htm

(p. 200) **Every Brain is Different**
"Brain Imaging Showing Individual Differences," Center for Applied Science Technology (CAST), old.cast .org/tesmm/example2_3/brain.htm

(p. 200) **Universal Design and Universal Design for Learning**
Elaine Ostroff, Molly Story and Beth Tauke, "About Universal Design," Universal Design Education Online, www.udeducation.org/learn/ aboutud.asp

(p. 202) **Including Students with Disabilities**
J. Pivik, J. McComas and M. Laflamme, "Barriers and facilitators to inclusive education as reported by students with physical disabilities and their parents," *Exceptional Children* 69, no. 1 (2002), www .questia.com/googleScholar.qst ?docId=5000643965

(p. 202) **Including Designers with Disabilities**
John D. Kemp, *Foreword to Building a World Fit For People: Designers with Disabilities at Work,* by Elaine Ostroff, Mark Limont and Daniel G. Hunter, Boston: Adaptive Environments Center, 2002.

(p. 204) **Features of an Inclusive Play Environment**
Inclusive Outdoor Learning Environments: an introductory guide, Utah State University's Center for Persons with Disabilities, 2003, www.beyondaccess.org/tutorials/ introductory%20guide.pdf

(p. 206) **High Point School**
"No Barriers to Fun, Friendship on Boundless Playgrounds," W.K. Kellogg Foundation, www.wkkf.org/ default.aspx?tabid=55&CID=318& ProjCID=318&ProjID=89&NID=28 &LanguageID=0

(p. 210) **Building Schools for the Learning Generation**
Richard W. Riley, "Creating America's First Learning Generation: NCTAF Symposium, July 10, 2005," National Commission on Teaching and America's Future (NCTAF), www.nctaf.org

(p. 213) **Velbert School for Educational Support and Counseling**
"Quality Indicators" and "Special Needs Education," © UNESCO 2009, used with permission from United Nations Educational Scientific and Cultural Organization, www.portal.unesco.org/education/ en/ev.php-URL_ID=11895&URL _DO=DO_TOPIC&URL_SECTION =201.html

(p. 214) **Velbert School for Educational Support and Counseling**
"Lebens- und Lernraum Schule," Montag Stiftungen, www.montag -stiftungen.com/foerderschule -velbert/

8 Rewired Learning

(p. 220) **From top to bottom**
Amanda Lenhart, Mary Madden and Paul Hitlin, *Teens and Technology: Youth are Leading the Transition to a Fully Wired and Mobile Nation,* PEW Internet & American Life Project, 2005, www.scribd .com/doc/15003/Teens-and -Technology-PEW-Internet-2005

Donald F. Roberts, Ulla G. Foehr and Victoria Rideout, *Generation M: Media in the Lives of 8–18 Year-olds,* The Henry J. Kaiser Family Foundation, 2005, www.kff .org/entmedia/upload/Generation

-M-Media-in-the-Lives-of-8-18-Year -olds-Report.pdf

A European Research Project: The Appropriation of New Media by Youth, Mediappro, with the support of the European Commisssion, Safer Internet Action Plan, 2006, www.mediappro.org/ publications/finalreport.pdf

Digest of Education Statistics, 2003, National Center for Education Statistics, in *The Internet at School,* by Paul Hitlin and Lee Rainie, PEW Internet & American Life Project, 2005, www.pew internet.org/pdfs/PIP_Internet _and_schools_05.pdf

Nic Covey, "46% of U.S. Tweens Use a Cell Phone, Nielsen Reports," Nielsen Mobile, www .nielsenmobile.com/html/press %20releases/MobileKids.html

Education Indicators in Canada: Report of the Pan-Canadian Education Indicators Program 2005, Statistics Canada, 2006, www.statcan.gc.ca/pub/81-582 -x/2006001/pdf/4225856-eng .pdf

Amanda Lenhart et al., *Writing, Technology and Teens,* PEW Internet & American Life Project, 2008, www.pewInternet.org/pdfs/ PIP_Writing_Report_FINAL3.pdf

Paul Hitlin and Lee Rainie, *The Internet at School,* PEW Internet & American Life Project, 2005, www.pewInternet.org/pdfs/PIP _Internet_and_schools_05.pdf

(p. 221) **From top to bottom**
Paul Hitlin and Lee Rainie, *The Internet at School,* PEW Internet & American Life Project, 2005, www.pewInternet.org/pdfs/PIP _Internet_and_schools_05.pdf

Seymour Papert interviewed by Dan Schwartz, "Ghost in the Machine: Seymour Papert on How Computers Fundamentally Change the Way Kids Learn," reprinted on One Laptop Per Child, learning .laptop.org/?q=node/28

Amanda Lenhart, Mary Madden and Paul Hitlin, *Teens and Technology: Youth are Leading the Transition to a Fully Wired and Mobile Nation,* PEW Internet & American Life Project, 2005, www.scribd.com/doc/15003/ Teens-and-Technology-PEW -Internet-2005

Paul Hitlin and Lee Rainie, *The Internet at School,* PEW Internet &

American Life Project, 2005, www.pewInternet.org/pdfs/PIP _Internet_and_schools_05.pdf

Edutopia staff, "12 Million: Teen Content Creators," *Edutopia, The George Lucas Educational Foundation* (February 2006), www .edutopia.org/12-million

Alvin Toffler, *Future Shock,* Toronto: Bantam Books, 1971.

Donald F. Roberts, Ulla G. Foehr and Victoria Rideout, *Generation M: Media in the Lives of 8–18 Year-olds,* The Henry J. Kaiser Family Foundation, 2005, www .kff.org/entmedia/upload/ Generation-M-Media-in-the-Lives -of-8-18-Year-olds-Report.pdf

(p. 228) **Space: The Classroom of the Future**
Crystal Bloemen and Penny Glackman (Coalition for Space Exploration, Education Advisory Board), "Space: a classroom for the future?," *The Denver Post,* August 20, 2007.

(p. 230) **Erma Ora Byrd Center for Educational Technologies**
"Challenger Center: Mission Simulations," Challenger Learning Centers, www.challenger.org/clc/ simulations.cfm

(p. 230) **Tonypandy Comprehensive School**
Tony Trainor, "Laser cutter is school's launch pad to future," *Western Mail,* December 14, 2001.

(p. 232) **Lake Geneva Middle School**
John K. Waters, "A Movable Feast," *T.H.E. Journal (1105 Media Inc.)* (December 2007), www.thejournal .com/articles/21715

(p. 232) **The School of the Future**
Julie Hall, "Design Trends," *American School & University* (January 1, 2007), © 2007 Penton Media. All rights reserved. www.asumag. com/mag/university_design _trends/index.html

(p. 234) **From Blackboard to Whiteboard, the Sky's the Limit**
(top) Rob Meissner, "Interactive Whiteboards," *School Planning & Management* (November 2006), www2.peterli.com/spm/ resources/articles/archive .php?article_id=1228

(p. 236) **Denver School of Science and Technology**
Andrew Zucker and Sarah Hug, *A Study of the 1:1 Laptop Program at the Denver School of Science*

& *Technology,* Denver School of Science and Technology, 2007, dsst.colorado.edu/documents/ Technology/DSST_Laptop_Study _Report.pdf

(p. 240) **Ingenium**
Peter Cowley, *Ingenium: BETT 07 Edition,* Ingenium, www.ingenium .org.uk

Image Sources

(p. 2) Harry Choi / BMD
(p. 4) © Michael Chrisman
(p. 6) © 2008 Blacklight Studios / Flickr
(p. 8) Courtesy of Bron Veale / Flickr
(p. 10) © Michael Chrisman
(p. 23) Courtesy of Daniel Ehrenworth, Oliver Eisenhuth, and Sarah Lewert
(p. 24) © Randy Faris/Veer Incorporated
(p. 26) Courtesy of Nancy Garcia/ Flickr
(p. 36) © Leah -Anne Thompson / Fotolia
(p. 40) © 2008 Crescent Manufacturing
(p. 42) Courtesy of OWP/P Architects
(p. 44–46) © Nigel Young / Foster and Partners
(p. 48) Courtesy of Daniel Ehrenworth
(p. 50) © Steven Errico / Veer Incorporated
(p. 52) © istockphoto.com / blackred
(p. 54) © 2007 Kurt Fischer / Usable
(p. 60) Knowledge (Harvard School of Education)
(p. 62) © Gillian Lynne / Lean Two Productions
(p. 66) From the Collections of the Henry Ford
(p. 68) © 2008 The George Lucas Educational Foundation (all rights reserved)
(p. 70–72) Courtesy of OWP/P Architects
(p. 74) Courtesy of Oliver Eisenhuth
(p. 76) © Veer Incorporated
(p. 78) © istockphoto.com / cscredon
(p. 86) Courtesy of VS Furniture
(p. 88) Courtesy of OWP/P Architects
(p. 90) © James Steinkamp Photography
(p. 92) © Martine Hamilton Knight / Anthony McGuirk (and team) / BDP Ltd. (Jarvis)
(p. 94) Courtesy of Trung Le / OWP/P

(p. 98–100) Courtesy of VS Furniture
(p. 100: left) Courtesy of Dr. Dieter Breithecker \ HABA Family GmbH
(p. 100: right) Coutesy of Dr. Dieter Breithecker \ Richter playgrounds (Spielgeräte GmbH)
(p. 102) Courtesy of Sarah Lewert
(p. 104) Courtesy of Dominic Harris / Flickr
(p. 106) © Warren Morgan / Veer Incorporated
(p. 116) Courtesy of Gary Wilson Photo/Graphic and Dull Olson Weekes Architects
(p. 118) © Peter Huebner, Christoph Forster, Olaf Huebner / plus+ bauplanung GmbH
(p. 120) © Ross Miller / Boston Schoolyard Initiative
(p. 124) © Benjamin Benschneider
(p. 128) © 2008 Google
(p. 130) © James Steinkamp Photography
(p. 132) Courtesy of Daniel Ehrenworth
(p. 134) © Michael Chrisman
(p. 136) © istockphoto.com / triggermouse
(p. 146) © Pir II Arkitektkontor AS
(p. 148) © Halkin Photography LLC
(p. 154) Courtesy of Robert Llewellyn
(p. 156–158) © Lara Swimmer Photography
(p. 160) Courtesy of Oliver Eisenhuth
(p. 162) © Veer Incorporated
(p. 164) Courtesy of Amanda Happé / Bruce Mau Design
(p. 168) © Carrie Branovan / Organic Valley Family of Farms
(p. 172: left) © The Edible Schoolyard
(p. 172: right) Courtesy of Haworth Primary School; Bradford, U.K.
(p. 178: middle row; left to right) © James Steinkamp Photography, © istockphoto.com / travelif, © istockphoto.com / webdata
(p. 178: bottom row) Harry Choi / BMD
(p. 180) © James Steinkamp Photography
(p. 182) Courtesy of David Sobel
(p. 184–186) © Arkitema K/S
(p. 188) Courtesy of Sarah Lewert
(p. 190) © Veer Incorporated
(p. 192) © istockphoto.com / TokenPhoto
(p. 198) © Meiko Tekechi Arquillos
(p. 200) Courtesy of CAST
(p. 206) Courtesy of Boundless Playgrounds
(p. 212–214) © Lukas Roth / Roland Dorn Architekt

(p. 217) Courtesy of OWP/P Architects
(p. 218) © Michael Prince / Veer Incorporated
(p. 220) © istockphoto.com / Amorphis
(p. 228) © NASA
(p. 230) Courtesy of the Center for Educational Technologies
(p. 234) Courtesy of VS Furniture
(p. 236) Courtesy of the American Architectural Foundation
(p. 238–240) © Peter Cowley / Ingenium
(p. 255) Courtesy of Trung Le / OWP/P

ACKNOWLEDGMENTS

OWP/P Architects

John Syvertsen with Story Bellows, Rick Dewar, Elizabeth Han, Chris Lambert, Trung Le, Kerry Leonard, Sarah Lewert, Pam Raymond, Alissa Remenschneider, Kelsey Salmen, Elias Vavaroutsos

VS Furniture

Dr. Thomas Müller with Carmen Braun, Christine DeBrot, Dr. Axel Haberer, Audrey Harvey, Claudius Reckord, Helen Hirsh Spence (as educational consultant)

Bruce Mau Design

Bruce Mau with Angelica Fox, interviewer, writer and editor; Chris Braden, Monica Bueno, Kim England, Paul Kawai, Erik Krim, Marc Lauriault, Kristina Ljubanovic, Judith McKay, Julie Bryn Netley, Pamela Olmstead, Elva Rubio, Carolina Söderholm, Laura Stein, Michael Waldin

Workshop Participants

Ogden Jr. Public School
Madelaine Allan (principal), Margie Kwan-Kirton (teacher)
students: Marwa Al Waeal, Bao Ming Chen, Malcolm Cole, Ricky Huang, Eva Jiang, Michelle Jin, Brandon Kirton, Keyn Le, ManXin Shi, Chih Li Wang, Rejean Wei, Timkin Yim, Heng Cheng Yu

Chicago School of the Arts
Pamela Jordan (head of school)
students: Gabe Abeyta, Kevin Beverley, Heather Day, Erika Dickerson, Merril Doty, Andrew Dwyer, Caitlin Foster, Monica George, Chelsea Gulbransen, Isabela Iatarola, Garth Johnson, Seth Kaplan, Kendel Kennedy, Madeline Kettlewell, Sae Jun Kim, Candace Leone, Matt McKeon, Joe Montesanto, Arielle Palmer, Matt Pino, Annemarie Pulaski, Clariza Saint George, Nikolas Spayne, Ivaila Veleva, Nina-Rose Wardanian, Lauren Williams

Robert Jungk Secondary School
Dr. Ruth Garstka (principal), Ms. Kuhlmann and Ms. Schmitz (teachers)
students: Lena Bischoff, Justine Deckert, Björn Engwicht, Sebastian Hartung, Jamie Heim, Allison Johnson, Matthieu Kalisch, Enes Kilic, René Kocsis, Jonas Leibovici, Jacqueline Liserre, Stefanie Ludwig, Jeffrey Meißner, Sophie Polack, Nikola Radusin,

Patrick Retzios, Sven Ruszynski, Reinhold Schüsser, Claudius Shoesmith-Bock, Marc-Fabian Stiehm, HeyNga Tang, Sinem Ucar, Kimberly Wojtynek, Daniel Ziebart

London Bridge
Peter Brown, Rick Dewar, Ty Goddard, Stephen Heppell, Trung Le, Gareth Long, Dr. Thomas Müller, Helen Hirsh Spence, Shelagh Wright

Thank you to all the architects, educators, schools, community groups, experts, and children who have contributed to the book. Special thanks to:

Eleanor Baxter, Victoria Bergsagel, Amy Erin Borovoy, Dr. Dieter Breithecker, Peter Brown, Nínive Calegari, Marie Castaneda-Toca, Mike Vietti Raffi Cavoukian, Esther Choi, Ann Cooper, Peter Cowley, James Dyson, Rosanne Ferruggia, Peter Hübner, Camille Humphrey, Keegan Humphrey, Elizabeth Larouer, Anthony McGuirk, Ross Miller, Glandina Morris, Jane Neuenschwander, Elaine Ostroff, André Jordan Padmore, Sir Ken Robinson, Michelle Sakayan, Linda Sarate, Calla Söderholm, David Sobel, Bill Strong, Karen Sutherland, David Suzuki, Audrey Taylor, Isabel Taylor, Kathryn Tollervey, Jenni Woolums, Janis Worklan

Print Information

Book Design: Bruce Mau Design

Pre-Press and Printing: Type A Print Inc.

Printed on: Mohawk Options, PC 100. FSC-certified. Made with 100% postconsumer waste (PCW). Manufactured with windpower. Process Chlorine free (PCF)

Copyedited by: Jayne Brown

Typeset by: Richard Hunt

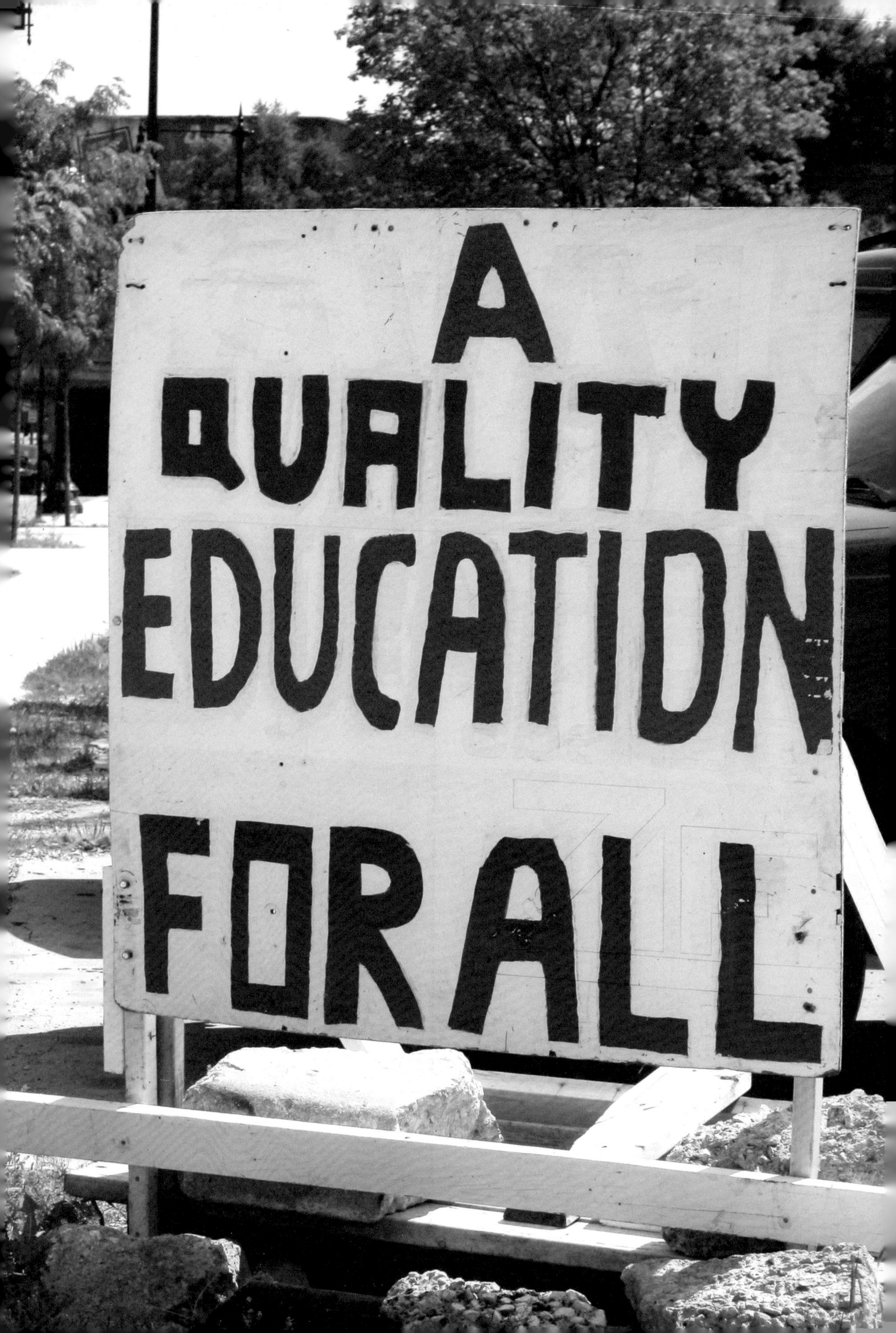
A
QUALITY
EDUCATION
FOR ALL